THE LYNDON JOHNSON STORY

THE
LYNDON JOHNSON
STORY

by BOOTH MOONEY

FARRAR, STRAUS AND CUDAHY
New York

Dedicated, in friendship, to
WALTER JENKINS
and all other members of the Johnson office staff

FOREWORD

I have always wondered why people say what they do when they write "forewords." It has been something of a mystery to me why forewords exist anyway. And I can think of nothing that would make even the most hardened extrovert more self-conscious than to write the foreword to a book about himself.

I have read enough forewords to know there are certain disclaimers that one must conventionally make. These usually appear in the first two or three paragraphs. In this field I am no trail-blazer and I therefore tread the traditional path. It so happens that while my disclaimers are conventional, they also are true.

This book is, then, no "authorized biography." At the age of forty-seven I am not yet old enough to feel the twinges (which I gather come eventually to every public man) to "set the record straight." I have always suspected, to put it bluntly, this means to make sure that the public man's side of the story is told as favorably as possible! Nor is it a habit of Texans to look back. We have a tradition of looking forward and not looking back to see where we have been or who is following us. There is time enough for that when we are gone.

I also accept the next conventional gambit, to be found in all standard "forewords." The subject of the biography, after pointing out that it is not "authorized" and, even going so far as to pretend that he is really not interested in a book written about himself, then goes on to say that, nevertheless, the author knows what he is writing about.

This also happens to be true. Booth Mooney has recently been subjected to three years of living with Lyndon Johnson, under every sort of strain and under all circumstances. He was once one of my political enemies and has become my personal friend. Of this I am proud, and this, I think, is a pride a reasonable man may take pleasure in. Booth was a member of my staff in Washington for three years. Above and beyond that, he is a Texan steeped in the traditions of Texas, and with a writer's eye for observing and understanding the effect upon and the bonds and the strength which the Lone Star State gives to her sons.

In short, he knows Texas, and he knows Washington, and, from personal experience, he knows that incredibly complex and extraordinarily superb invention of free democratic government—the United States Senate, of which I am at the moment Majority Leader.

I hope the reader will like this book. I have read it and I like it. I would have said a lot of things differently, much of it I would have taken out, for what are, essentially, I suppose, selfish reasons, and I would have stressed a number of other things which the author did not. But on the whole I liked it very much and I have long ago learned that Lyndon Johnson's view of Lyndon Johnson is not really the right one or even the desirable one. I feel that if the book is at all out of perspective, it is because Booth Mooney has been too kind. This is an error of friendship, the most easily forgiven of all the sins, and I know of no man in public life, including this one, who is so academic as to pitch a quarrel on such a pleasant ground as this.

Since I still have the Floor, there is one further word I want to say on behalf of Lyndon Johnson. It is no secret, I imagine, that I am a Democrat. I will always be one. It is, first of all, my heritage and my legacy from my forebears. All of the Johnsons and all of the Baineses have been Democrats from time immemorial.

But I feel quite strongly those of you who may happen to read this book and who do not know me, should understand that the fact I am a Democrat is not simply a matter of geography or birth or of Texas tradition. I admit I was born lucky but after 26 years of public life I have learned intellectually and from experience that it is lucky to be born a Democrat.

To put it simply, I am a Democrat by conviction. The Democratic Party has more to offer to the successive generations of this nation than has the other party. Under its broad tent and flying banners people of many interests and many sections have always united and, I hope most fervently, will always be able to unite.

The other party has always been the party of a single interest. This single interest, by which I mean Business, is a legitimate interest, and it is one which has contributed mightily to the growth of the United States. It has a right to and deserves national representation. And there is room for it, or part of it, in the Democratic Party. But it can be only one of many interests. There its rights and privileges, and its duties, are considered alongside those of the farmer and rancher, the working man and the various rights and aspirations of the different sections of the country, including, of course, those of Texas.

Lyndon B. Johnson

THE LYNDON JOHNSON STORY

· I ·

Lyndon Baines Johnson, Majority Leader of the United
States Senate, suffered a coronary occlusion on July 2,
1955. The heart attack opened the way for the final
stage of a metamorphosis that had transformed a brash
young congressman from the brash state of Texas into,
first, a politicians' politician in the tradition-ridden Senate and, eventually, a people's politician in the United
States of America.

There had been no advance warning of the heart
attack—at least none that Johnson recognized or admitted—and there was little more previous notice of the
changed status that Johnson had come to occupy in the
popular mind.

Johnson's seizure came dramatically near the end of
a congressional session he had dominated. It focused
nationwide attention on him and on the accomplishments of the Senate under his leadership.

Although numerous individuals knew of Johnson's
prowess as a legislative leader, his full stature was not
generally recognized during the final days of June, 1955,
as the first session of the Eighty-fourth Congress proceeded to deal with the business at hand.

In the Senate, this business went forward smoothly and rapidly under the generalship of the hard-driving Majority Leader.

The majority he led was razor-edge thin. Forty-nine Senators sat on the Democratic side of the Senate chamber. That number included Wayne Morse of Oregon, who had been elected as a Republican but now was aligned with the Democrats. In the seats across the aisle dividing the two parties were forty-seven Republicans, who could be joined in the case of a tie vote by a Republican Vice-President, presiding officer of the Senate.

Under such circumstances it would not have been surprising if things had bogged down completely in the Senate. Nothing of the kind happened. In *Newsweek* for June 27, Samuel Shaffer of the magazine's Washington bureau reported: "One day last week the U. S. Senate passed ninety bills, confirmed an ambassador and a Federal Trade Commissioner and then knocked off because it had temporarily run out of business. The elapsed time: Four hours and forty-three minutes."

This may have looked easy to someone not familiar with the procedure by which the Senate has thoroughly earned its reputation as the greatest *deliberative* body in the world. It was not easy, but it was possible. And it was possible only because of the day-and-night efforts of a man whose actions were guided by an admonition contained in the Book of Isaiah: "Come now, and let us reason together."

Lyndon Johnson quoted that admonition often to

other members of the Senate during the first six months of 1955.

Johnson was not yet forty-seven years old. He had behind him only one full term of service in the Senate, where the feeling about seniority smacks of ancestor worship. Yet on vital issues he carried along with him, in a body which has been said by some observers to be composed of ninety-six jealous prima donnas, men much older both in years and experience.

He represented the conservative state of Texas, which had favored the Eisenhower-Nixon ticket in 1952. Some of the liberal members of his own party considered him a rank tory. Some of his own constituents thought of him as a dangerous left-wing radical. Yet he had brought together in the Senate the divergent elements of the Democratic Party, while steadfastly refusing to lead partisan attacks on the program of the Republican Administration.

He rarely made formal speeches on the floor of the Senate. When he did deliver an address it was not as an accomplished orator but rather as a straightforward man talking straightforwardly about matters that he made simple and understandable. Yet it was Johnson that the knowing newsmen and newswomen watched and listened to most attentively from the press gallery above, and whom they approached for information about the significance of what was going on in the Senate.

What the reporters saw, looking down on Johnson from the press gallery, was a man constantly in action, and everything Johnson did had a meaning.

He leaned across the aisle from his Senate seat to whisper earnestly to Senator William F. Knowland of California, his opposite number among the Republicans. It took only a moment. But the experienced reporters knew the way was being cleared for quick action on a legislative measure that under different circumstances, under different leadership, could have stalled the Senate for days.

He got to his feet and obtained the recognition of the presiding officer, as he did many times daily in his capacity as Majority Leader. He spoke a few words, his Texas drawl hardly audible in the Senate chamber, and then sat down abruptly. As he replaced his thick-lensed glasses, the process set in motion by his words would be speeding another piece of legislative business to completion.

He raised his dark head alertly as a Democratic Senator approached his desk for a brief conference. The conference ended with an exchange of nods. The reporters could expect to find that Senator voting alongside Johnson on the next important issue, no matter how controversial.

He jerked his six-foot-three, two-hundred-pound frame out of his chair to walk briskly from the Senate chamber into the Democratic cloakroom. Vigilant observers above realized his departure was not merely for the purpose of giving him a chance to smoke a cigarette, although he was a chain smoker and people do not smoke on the floor of the United States Senate. He would, the reporters knew, be hard at it in the cloakroom: praising a colleague for his work in committee, arguing persuasively with a Southern conservative about a housing bill or minimum wage legislation, inducing two Senators who stood at opposite poles on almost all issues to advance toward each other on a specific issue.

Johnson's most effective work was done in the cloakrooms or in his private office. He was a master of the personal approach. "Being won over by Johnson," Mary McGrory of the Washington *Star* once wrote, "is a rather overwhelming experience."

"The full treatment," Miss McGrory continued, "is an incredibly potent mixture of persuasion, badgering, flattery, threats, reminders of past favors and future advantages. It accounts for Johnson's enormous effectiveness in a small room with a small group."

There was a little more to it than that, of course. When Johnson approached another Senator to talk about a legislative measure, he was armed with the pertinent facts. He does not neglect his homework on either issues or personalities. He learns by asking questions and then listening, really listening, to the answers. When he has all the facts, he throws the full weight of his compelling personality into presenting them to others.

This was a man with a purpose, simple in nature, if not always easy of execution. Johnson wanted Senators to work together for the national good.

That term "national good" meant many things to him. It meant welfare legislation for the benefit of needy old people. It meant governmental action to assure that

[7]

a fair share of the national income was received by farmers. It meant decent minimum wages for working men and women, a strong system of national defense, a realistic approach to problems in the field of international relations, fair treatment for minority groups.

These were some of the aims Johnson had sought to achieve long before he attained leadership in the United States Senate. Now he was in a position to do more than ever about the causes he knew in his heart and mind were right.

The press, radio and television representatives on Capitol Hill were the first to tell the country that the Senate had the hardest-working Majority Leader in its history. They told that story repeatedly during the month of June, 1955. Gould Lincoln, veteran Washington political writer, headed one of his columns, LYNDON JOHNSON MOVES MOUNTAINS. Doris Fleeson, liberal newspaper columnist who as often as not criticized Johnson severely, wrote after one exhibition of his leadership that the only thing left to him was to set his next triumph in the Senate to music.

Members of the Senate woke up to the fact that the body was doing far more than the legislative norm, and seemingly with much less than normal effort.

Senators holding such disparate views as Harry Flood Byrd of Virginia and Hubert Humphrey of Minnesota rose on the floor of the Senate to pay their respects to the leadership that was making this record possible. Stuart Symington of Missouri declared Johnson was "establishing a record for legislative efficiency in handling the business of the Senate and the problems of the country which may be unequalled in the history of the Senate."

On July 1, which was to turn out to be Johnson's last day in action in the Senate during that session, one colleague after another spoke glowingly of his work.

Mike Mansfield of Montana said that the Majority Leader, in "establishing a record of cooperation and accomplishment which is setting a fine mark for all to see," had earned "the gratitude and thanks of the President of the United States for the spirit of cooperation and the high statesmanship he has shown."

John Stennis of Mississippi, representing a state as far removed from Montana as possible in political tradition and philosophy, agreed. "I reflect no more than what I think is the unanimous opinion of the members of the entire Senate," he said, "when I say that the Senator from Texas has labored long, ably, and effectively to carry out what I call a patriotic program, without any label on it of party or partisanship."

South Carolina's Olin Johnston summed up the sentiment of Democratic Senators, and perhaps that of some Republicans, when he said that, under Johnson's leadership, "we have been able to accomplish the almost impossible, and to do it in record time." Along with that statement, the South Carolina Senator inserted in the *Congressional Record* a list of forty-nine outstanding legislative accomplishments of the session.

Johnson was proud of these accomplishments. But the goals he set for himself taxed his strength to the utmost.

He was not in peak physical condition anyway, for he had not given himself sufficient time to recover fully from a kidney stone operation undergone back in January.

He was working too hard, but then he had always worked harder than most men. His day began at seven-thirty in the morning and rarely ended before midnight. It was work all the way. Never enthusiastic about the social game, he had reduced his participation in it almost to the vanishing point.

There had been no night meetings of the Senate, as there customarily are in the concluding weeks of a session. Johnson had said repeatedly that night sessions should be avoided, if at all possible, in order to conserve the energies and safeguard the health of the members. The sound rule he made for others he did not apply to himself. He was still in his office, endlessly conferring, at eleven o'clock more nights than not, telephoning, studying digests of legislative bills, planning floor strategy for the next day or the next week.

Even the most conscientious members of the United States Senate, with very few exceptions, take some time to enjoy the social whirl of the nation's capital. Johnson had never done much socializing. As Majority Leader, he did virtually none.

One midnight he came home dog-tired from a late session of the Senate. His wife had just come in from a dance. She gave a glowing report of the evening's pleasures.

"I don't see why you can't take some time off for fun,

Lyndon," she expostulated. "All the other Senators do. Why, Senator ———, who is so much older than you, was there and having a fine time. I danced with him twice."

"Senator ———!" Her husband exploded into laughter. "Why, it was passing his pet bill through the Senate that kept me at work so late tonight."

Johnson was well aware that if it had not been this particular bill it would have been something else. There was always something.

He was tired all the time, even when exhilarated by the knowledge that things were going so well in the Senate. One morning late in June, riding into town with his younger brother, Sam Houston Johnson, up from Texas for a visit, he said, "Sam Houston, if I can just get through this session I'm going to take things easy on the ranch the rest of the year. If I can just make it to the end of the session."

He was no more tired than usual on Friday, July 1. *July 1.* The Senate session was short, ending in the early afternoon to enable the members to start the long Independence Day week-end. Johnson was at his desk throughout. He responded briefly and modestly to the tributes paid him by several colleagues. He made one of his rare speeches, talking of President Eisenhower's announced decision to take another look at the controversial Dixon-Yates power plant contract. Johnson predicted, correctly, that this would prove to be the next to the last step toward cancellation of the contract.

After the Senate adjourned, he spent the remainder of

[11]

the afternoon at work in his office. He instructed his staff to take time off until Tuesday morning. "Let's get in good shape for this final drive," he told his top aides. "We've got a lot to do in the next month." He said he planned to come to the office for a while Saturday, but he would merely be telephoning and would not need anybody around.

He had dinner late that night with his old friends, House Speaker Sam Rayburn and Senator Symington. They talked at length about the prospect of adjournment by July 30, a goal Johnson was determined to meet. Rayburn and Symington cautioned him, the Speaker in rather blunt language, about knocking himself out with the tremendous effort he was exerting to make the session one of the most notable in Senate history.

"I'm tired," he admitted. "But I am all right. Anyway, I'm going to rest this week-end. Sunday and Monday at least."

A few Senators were still in town Saturday. Johnson talked to some of them about the Senate program for the coming week. His brother came in to have lunch with him. Johnson told him he planned to spend the week-end at George Brown's home in Middleburg, Virginia. Brown was an old and close friend from Texas.

In the afternoon, Johnson held an informal news conference in his office with some of his friends from the press gallery. Two of the wire service reporters were trying to write their stories for Tuesday so they could be free for the week-end. They depended on Johnson to tell them what might be expected to happen in the Senate the following week.

On the way down to Middleburg in the early evening, Johnson began to feel a constriction in his chest. He complained that indigestion was giving him heartburn. After a while he asked Norman Edwards, his driver, to make sure the car's air conditioning unit was working properly.

"I can't seem to breathe," he said.

The driver checked. The air conditioning was all the way on. They tried opening the windows. That did no good.

"I feel nauseated, Norman," Johnson complained. "I hope I'm not going to be sick."

He said nothing more then, leaning back in the car and rubbing his chest with one hand, until they arrived at George Brown's place. He asked Edwards to wait for a while, saying he might have to go back to Washington.

Half an hour later, Johnson came out and told the driver to return without him. It was arranged that Edwards would bring Mrs. Johnson down to Middleburg the next day. Johnson felt better; he told Edwards he had taken some baking soda and believed he was going to be all right.

But he was not all right. His car was hardly out of sight before the pain returned to his chest. Brown, not bothering to hide his anxiety, called a local physician. The doctor came immediately. He said, with some hesitancy, that the symptoms could be those of a heart attack.

Johnson characteristically took charge at once. "If you think it might be a heart attack, let's act like we *know* it's a heart attack," he said.

The telephoning began, but this time not with the Senator doing it. An ambulance was called to take Johnson to Bethesda Naval Hospital, just outside Washington. The hospital was notified. So were Mrs. Johnson and two or three members of the Senator's staff. Calls went out to heart specialists and personal friends on the staff of Mayo Clinic.

On the ambulance ride to the hospital, Johnson asked the doctor accompanying him for a cigarette.

"Unless I'm mistaken," said the doctor, "you're through with cigarettes for all time."

Johnson grinned. "Don't say that, Doctor. Take away my seniority in the Senate, but don't take me off my three packs a day."

He worried, as they rode, about spoiling the ambulance driver's Saturday night. "I sure appreciate this," he said several times. "It's sure good of you."

Mostly, though, he did not talk. He thought of the time he had almost died of pneumonia in the Far East during the war. He remembered the emergency appendectomy he had undergone years before, the flight from Texas to Mayo's in Rochester, Minnesota, in the middle of the toughest political campaign he had ever known, the operation a few months before for the removal of kidney stones. Those had been bad times.

This might be worse, he knew, than any of those experiences. This might be the worst thing he had ever come up against.

At the hospital, with doctors and nurses about and with his wife standing over him, he said, "Before you put me under that oxygen tent, I want three minutes with three people. They're all here. I saw them in the corridor. It will do me more harm if I don't talk to them than if I do."

The three were Felton Johnston, Secretary of the Senate; George Reedy, staff member of the Democratic Policy Committee, of which Johnson was chairman; and Walter Jenkins, his most trusted aide.

He told Felton Johnston to telephone Earle Clements, Kentucky Senator and, as Democratic Whip, second in command on the Senate floor, to tell him he would be Acting Leader for the remainder of the session. "Tell him I won't be back this session," Johnson said. "Even if I get well."

To Reedy, who handled his press contacts, he said: "Call the wire services and tell them I've had a heart attack. Tell them the doctors say it is moderately severe. Don't try to play it down. Just tell them the facts."

To Jenkins: "My money clip's in my coat pocket. Take it. Lady Bird will be needing cash right away. If things don't turn out all right, my will is in the safe at the office. Take care of things, Walter."

He turned his suddenly haggard face back toward his wife. "Stay with me," he said.

He took her hand in his as the doctor approached.

"All right," he said. "I'm ready now."

Within minutes he went into shock. Some of the best medical men in the country worked throughout the night on the seventeenth floor of the Naval Hospital to keep the breath of life in his body.

· II ·

———————

In the early afternoon of Sunday, August 27, 1908, an elderly gentleman mounted a horse on his farm near the Texas town he had founded and that bore his name. Sitting straight in the saddle, he set out to call on his neighbors in the rural community. To each of them he gave the same solemn message:

"A United States Senator was born this morning—my grandson."

The folks around Johnson City, Texas, knew Samuel Ealy Johnson, Sr. His word was good with them. So far as the homefolks were concerned, the destiny of the newest member of the Johnson family was set even before he had been given a name. Their faith was confirmed when the proud grandfather reiterated his judgment from time to time during the next few years, commenting to all who would listen on the boy's fine head, splendid eyes, precocity, determination and charm.

Lyndon Johnson was born to politics. His father served five terms in the Texas legislature. His maternal grandfather also saw service in the legislature as well as in the office of the Texas Secretary of State. His maternal grandmother was the niece of a man who signed the

Texas Declaration of Independence from Mexico, fought in the freedom-winning Battle of San Jacinto, and became a member of the First Congress of the Republic of Texas. One of that grandmother's uncles was a governor of Kentucky. Her forebears, back in the Old Country, for several generations represented their home district in the Scottish Parliament.

Sam Ealy Johnson, Jr., the father, was school teacher, farmer and legislator. He was first elected to the state legislature in 1904 when he was twenty-seven years old. He served two terms then and later was elected to three more two-year terms. During this latter service, which covered the period of World War I, he became well known in Texas as a result of a speech on tolerance he delivered in the House of Representatives. The speech was a fine plea that common sense and justice be applied to and combined with the wartime patriotism sweeping the country.

As a legislator, Sam Johnson was the author of numerous constructive measures. Early in his first term he successfully sponsored a bill appropriating funds to purchase the Alamo in San Antonio, shrine of Texas' war for independence. He wrote a bill providing for the erection of a home for the widows of Confederate veterans. He worked hard to help get farmers out of the mud with improved highways. He was a pioneer in leading the way to provide public funds to aid drought-stricken areas of the state.

One of Sam Johnson's early votes in the legislature was cast for a young man from North Texas who wanted to be Speaker of the Texas House. The youngster got the job. His name was Sam Rayburn.

Sam Johnson was married in August, 1907, to Rebekah Baines. She was the daughter of Joseph W. Baines, Johnson's predecessor as a representative in the state legislature. Sam had courted Rebekah by taking her to reunions of Confederate veterans to hear the oratory of Senators Joe Bailey and Charlie Culberson and Governor Tom Campbell. Once the young legislator had invited her to hear William Jennings Bryan orate with his free-silver tongue before the Texas legislature.

"Sam was enchanted," his wife said years later, "to find a girl who really liked politics."

Rebekah, a staunch and determined young woman who worked her way through her final year at Baylor College after her father suffered financial reverses, had been teaching classes in "expression" in Fredericksburg, county seat of Gillespie County. After their marriage, the couple moved out to the Johnson farm on the Pedernales River. It was there a year later that their first child, the one acclaimed by Grandpa Johnson as a future Senator, was born.

In the ancestral background of Lyndon Johnson were public servants, ministers, cattlemen, journalists, planters, schoolteachers, a college president, a co-founder of the Daughters of the American Revolution.

His grandfather, Samuel Ealy Johnson, Sr., was born in 1838 in Alabama, the tenth child of Jesse Johnson and Lucy Webb Barnett Johnson. Samuel Ealy's parents lived in Georgia most of their lives, moving to Texas in

1846. After the father died ten years later, young Sam and his brother Tom set themselves up in the cattle business. They bought cattle and pastured them in Gillespie County before driving them on to Kansas markets. In the late 'fifties the brothers established headquarters at what is now Johnson City. It was the first settlement in that section.

Samuel Ealy Johnson served through the Civil War. He was married in 1867 to Eliza Bunton, daughter of Robert Holmes Bunton and Jane MacIntosh Bunton. Eliza Bunton Johnson was a niece of John Wheeler Bunton, signer of the Texas Declaration of Independence and the Constitution of the Republic of Texas. It was he who served in the Republic's First Congress. It was another of Eliza's cousins, Mary Desha, who was co-founder of the DAR.

Rebekah Baines' father, Joseph Wilson Baines, was born in Louisiana in the middle 1840's, but was brought up and educated in Texas. He served in the Civil War. Schoolteacher and lawyer, he also established a weekly newspaper in McKinney, then later was Secretary of State and member of the legislature.

His father, George W. Baines, Sr., was a Baptist minister in Arkansas, Louisiana and, finally, Texas. He also served in a state legislature, that of Arkansas. He was editor of the first Baptist paper to be published in Texas. He became president of the denominational college, Baylor University, in 1861, resigning the following year because of ill health. George Baines was a good friend of the almost legendary Sam Houston.

Whatever else Lyndon Johnson inherited from these ancestors, he was without question bequeathed an enormous store of physical energy. According to his mother and others who knew him early, he was a dynamo from childhood.

He was a happy, active and healthy child. There were many things to do on a farm. Lyndon did them all. Under the watchful eye of a mother who had a dedicated sense of parental responsibility and under the careful guidance of a proud and intelligent father, the boy grew as fast as the jackrabbits that loped over the hills.

He was active mentally as well as physically. His mother began early to tell him stories from the Bible, history and mythology. Lyndon liked best the stories of actual occurrences. "Is it true?" he would demand of his mother. "Did it actually happen, Mama?"

Rebekah Baines Johnson taught him the alphabet from A-B-C blocks before he was two. By the time he was three he could recite all the Mother Goose rhymes and poems from Longfellow and Tennyson. At four he was reading for himself.

When he started to school at the age of five, however, it could not be said that he took readily to books. There were many things to do besides study and they were all more attractive.

Old report cards showed that his school grades generally were good, except in "deportment" where a "B" was as high as he could rise. His grades were due more to the persistence of his mother than to his own eagerness to learn. She knew she had a determined son, but her own determination was not in short supply. For every artifice Lyndon set up to dodge his studies, she found another that was effective in making him learn.

"Many times," she has said, "I would not catch up with the fact that Lyndon was not prepared on a lesson until breakfast time of a school day. Then I would get the book and put it on the table in front of his father and devote the whole breakfast period to a discussion with my husband of what my son should have learned the night before.

"Lyndon was too well trained to interrupt adult table talk. Forced to listen, he would learn. That way, and by following him to the front gate nearly every morning and telling him tales of history and geography and algebra, I could see that he was prepared for the work of the day."

In spite of the necessity of force-feeding knowledge to him, the parents were pleased with the way the boy developed initiative and resourcefulness. He rode the few miles to school on his own pony. He had a group of friends, all older than he, and he often brought one home to spend the night. He took very seriously his position as the oldest of the family of five children.

Lyndon was graduated from the Johnson City high school in the spring of 1924. He was president of his class of seven members. He and a friend won the debate competition in the county interscholastic league that year.

Graduation from high school meant to him a happy release from years of drudgery. He had no thought of college. He was finished with books. He wanted to get out into the world. He felt that he was a man, which he was in height, having sprung up to more than six feet, although he was as skinny as a country telephone pole.

His parents were eager for him to attend college. Just to make sure there would be no more talk of it, he organized five of his friends into an expedition to California. It could have been called running away from home.

The boy learned a great deal during the few months he was in California. He and his friends soon ran out of money. They separated to hunt jobs.

"That was the first time I went on a diet," he reported later. "Nothing to eat was the principal item on my food chart. Up and down the coast I tramped, washing dishes, waiting on tables, doing farm work when it was available, and always growing thinner."

There was a solution, of course, and that was to work and hitchhike his way back toward Texas and Johnson City. That is what the long, lanky youth finally did. He was very happy to get back home, but he still had no idea of going to college.

He landed a job on a road gang near Johnson City. He shoveled gravel and drove a truck and pushed a wheelbarrow. He grew calluses on his hands and did a reasonable amount of helling around on Saturday nights.

His mother, with characteristic persistence, pressed home to him at every opportunity the fact that work was honorable, whether with the hands or with the head. "But," she added, "education opens up everything."

Sam Johnson talked to his son about his job. "It's fine to be satisfied with the simple things. A man who is satisfied to be a laborer will never have much on his mind. Of course there won't be much in it either, but a man who is willing to devote all his life to a road job really doesn't need much."

Such talk eventually had its effect. So did the grinding monotony of the work he was doing.

One raw, cold evening, Lyndon came home from an especially hard day on the highway and announced, "I'm sick of working just with my hands. I don't know if I can work with my brain, but I'm ready to try. Mama, if you and Daddy can get me in college, I'll go as soon as I can."

His mother walked immediately to the telephone and called a family friend who was an official of Southwest Texas State Teachers College at San Marcos, a town some forty miles distant from Austin, the state capital. She arranged right then for her son to enter the college at the beginning of the next semester. That was in February, 1927.

There was little money. Lyndon went to the Johnson City bank and borrowed $75 on his own note to get started. At the college he got a job as janitor. Disliking the work, he set out to shorten as much as he could the time he would have to do it. He had no intention of spending four years in getting his degree. He was through with wasting time.

The young man who had scorned higher education now soaked up knowledge furiously. Working alone after other students had left, he recited his lessons aloud. He practiced oratory in the halls he swept. He learned to do the janitorial chores faster than they had ever been done before and used the time he saved to take on another job as secretary of the college president—and to study constantly.

Even then not all his energy was consumed. As many youths of his age turn to sports, he turned to debate and campus politics. He became the college's star debater. He had his first success in the political field when he organized a new faction, which he labeled the "White Stars," to wrest control of campus politics from the entrenched, athlete-dominated "Black Stars."

He edited the college newspaper and was a leader in numerous extra-curricular activities. His grades were excellent. He made numerous friends who would stay with him through the years.

Lyndon Johnson received his degree from Southwest Texas State Teachers College in August, 1930, when he was twenty-two years old. That was three and one-half years after he had entered the school. During this time he had completed three months of pre-college work and four full years of college work—and had taken time out to make needed money by teaching school one year in a small town in South Texas.

After his graduation from college, he joined the faculty of a high school in Houston to teach public speaking and debate. The school had many Latin-American students. Conflicts arose at times between them and the Anglo pupils. In ironing out these differences, the young teacher used and developed his talent for influencing people to get along among themselves.

He liked teaching and was good at it. The debate teams he advanced won honors for themselves in state competitions. He was popular with his students and with other faculty members.

But the family tradition of politics was much on his mind. When the opportunity came, late in the year 1931, to go to Washington as secretary to a Texas congressman, he jumped at it. One way or another, after that, he was always in politics.

· III ·

His entrance on the Washington scene was made under the aegis of Congressman Richard M. Kleberg, one of the owners of the fabulous King Ranch of Texas. Kleberg, wealthy and conservative in the Texas tradition, had been elected to the House of Representatives in a special election in November, 1931. Johnson had participated in Kleberg's campaign with speech-making and personal work with the voters, and the rancher had taken a fancy to the aggressive youngster.

It was a yeasty time of change in the nation's capital, a great time for a young, intelligent, politically-minded man to be in Washington. Especially if he were a Democrat.

Herbert Hoover was in the White House and the Republicans still controlled the Senate, but the Democrats had captured the House of Representatives in the 1930 elections. Political observers took it for granted that the Hoover Administration would be swept completely out of power in the 1932 general election. The Democrats were making big plans for the time when they would finish taking over the government. Already, new Federal agencies were being set up in an effort to check the disastrous economic depression that had the country in its grip.

This milieu of exciting ideas and excited people was just right for Johnson. He realized at once that Washington was the place for him. He embarked on a studied effort to make it his town.

Arthur Perry, at that time secretary to Senator Tom Connally of Texas and already well versed in the ways of Capitol Hill, recalls the newcomer made quite an impact on the group of established congressional secretaries.

"I remember when Dick Kleberg brought Lyndon around to our office and told me he wished I would teach his new secretary everything I knew and show him how to find his way around Washington," Perry said later. "Lyndon started asking questions as soon as he knew my name. He followed the same procedure with everyone else he met. He was out to learn all he could and learn it fast."

He did learn fast. "You never had to tell him anything a second time." Perry said. "This skinny boy was as green as anybody could be, but within a few months he knew how to operate in Washington better than some who had been here for twenty years before him."

Johnson, Perry and many other young men working as secretaries to congressmen lived in the Dodge Hotel on Capitol Hill. They were never far away from their jobs, in either body or spirit. When they were not actually at work, they were thinking or talking about work. Their ideas were as divergent as those of their bosses.

Their minds were eager and absorbent. They debated political issues at their meals, raised their voices in defense and in condemnation as they walked the few blocks from their offices to the hotel, crowded one another's rooms at night to express strong opinions on the state of the American government.

Lyndon Johnson was usually to be found in the midst of the group where arms were being waved most wildly and the talk was most violent. He did his share of the talking. He did more than his share of listening.

"When a group of us went to the cafeteria for lunch," Arthur Perry reports of those days, "Lyndon would be at the head of the line. He would grab a tray and pick out the food he wanted, hurry to a table and start wolfing his meal. Often—usually—by the time the rest of us reached the table he would have finished eating.

"That left him free to shoot questions at us while we ate. If he didn't like the answers he got, he would argue. Lyndon was the greatest argufier any of us had ever seen. It took me a long time to catch on to the fact that most of his arguing was done simply to bring out every possible answer to his arguments. He wanted to be sure he knew all the answers."

Johnson made friends. He was personable and gregarious. In argument, he could be devastating. In friendly conversation, he could be irresistible. Nor was his standing on "The Hill" damaged by the fact that his father's old friend, Sam Rayburn, rising to power in the House of Representatives, had taken him under his wing.

The congressional secretaries had their own organization, which they called the "Little Congress." Johnson had been in Washington for only a year when someone suggested casually that he offer himself as a candidate for Speaker of the Little Congress. The suggestion was hardly meant seriously, for the miniature congress operated under a rigid seniority system. Newcomers were supposed to listen and learn, just as was the custom for freshman members of the actual Congress.

The suggestion was no joke to the new secretary from Texas. He ran for the office and won it. He won the victory by the simple method of enlisting the aid of a few friends in signing up for membership the congressional secretaries who had never bothered to participate in the affairs of the Little Congress. Naturally, these new members were pledged to support Lyndon Johnson for Speaker. They swamped the entrenched Old Guard.

The New Deal was in full swing. Johnson loved the heady atmosphere of Washington as experiments with new concepts of government swept on. Like many other Americans, the Texan had a new hero in Franklin Delano Roosevelt. In those days, when all around him men were making the world over every morning before breakfast, was born Johnson's scorn of what he called "cain't do men." He saw many things done that timid men had said could not possibly be accomplished.

To be sure, his own official role in those events was bound by the confines of one congressional office. But he went to Dick Kleberg's office early and stayed there late. He learned all there was to know about running a congressman's office; how to get things done for the

[30]

folks back home; how to deal effectively with the government bureaus; how to get jobs for constituents and how to leave them feeling friendly toward their congressman when jobs were unobtainable.

He learned, too, who was powerful and therefore important in Congress, and how the powerful ones got that way. He saw at first hand how much it meant to attain seniority as a member of Congress. He absorbed knowledge from wise and experienced Sam Rayburn, and always he was everywhere asking questions.

Johnson got back to Texas for visits from time to time. He was in Austin in September, 1934, when he met the girl he knew at once he wanted to marry. Her name was Claudia Taylor, but a Negro nurse had nicknamed her "Lady Bird" when she was a baby and Lady Bird she had remained. She was the bright, charming and very pretty daughter of a well-to-do East Texas landowner and businessman.

Typically, Johnson asked her for a date only minutes after they had met. He had made up his mind. He saw no need for wasting time. But Miss Taylor was going back home to Marshall that night, so she declined.

Back in Washington he proceeded to lay down a barrage of telegrams, long distance telephone calls and letters. It was two months before he was able to get back to Texas. He at last had his date with Lady Bird and talked her into marrying him.

"Sometimes," his wife said reminiscently, some years later, "Lyndon simply takes your breath away."

They were married November 17, 1934, and went to

[31]

Mexico for their honeymoon. By the time they set up housekeeping in Washington, the fast-talking Texan knew he had won a double prize. He not only had the one possible wife for Lyndon Johnson but also had the ideal helpmate for a going-places politician.

The couple barely had time to get well settled in Washington before they were on the move again. In August, 1935, a few days before his twenty-seventh birthday, Johnson was appointed State Administrator for Texas of the National Youth Administration.

The NYA was one of the stars in the New Deal crown. Its purpose was as simple as it was praiseworthy: to get young Americans off the street corners and highways and put them to work, either in school or at jobs. In that depression-ridden time, thousands of youngsters were idle and without hope, many of them wandering aimlessly about the country, all of them constituting a threat rather than a promise to the future of the United States.

Since coming to Washington, Johnson had given much effort to helping his former pupils and college classmates. He had arranged for a number of them to obtain jobs in the capital. He had helped others to get work enabling them to attend college in Texas. He was a natural leader of young people.

Johnson was the youngest NYA State Administrator in the country. He was determined to be the best one. When he got off a plane in Austin to embark on his new work, he told newspaper reporters, "As I see it, my job is to work myself out of a job."

[32]

His efforts brought him his first taste of national fame. The organization he built in Texas was used as a model by many other states. He put thousands of youngsters to work on such projects as playgrounds, highway road-side parks and soil conservation. He pleaded the merits of his boys and girls to private employers. He urged college officials to see that their NYA apportionments were used effectively to give deserving and needy students a chance to complete their education.

In Texas, the National Youth Administration became a factor in the lives of some thirty thousand young men and women. Of these, eighteen thousand were given assistance in getting through high school and college; the other twelve thousand obtained jobs of one kind or another through the NYA.

"Those were the great days," Johnson said later. "Those kids came into the units as we established them, railing at fortune and circumstance and cowed by the economic conditions that had left them without jobs or the hope of jobs. After they came to us, their scowls were changed to smiles.

"For a time after we began to work I tried to be the first person on the job every morning, but I found that I had just set up a contest. They were as anxious to get there as I was. They were as anxious to show me that all they had lacked was opportunity as I was anxious to have them show it.

"Skills grew with practice. Opportunities came to them as they perfected these skills. If the Roosevelt Administration had never done another thing, it would have been justified by the work of this great institution for salvaging youth."

It was this attitude toward his work that earned for him from the National Director of the NYA the accolade that the young Texan did the best job of any State Administrator.

Naturally, Johnson derived immense personal satisfaction from his job. From the time he started his career as a schoolteacher he had a deep-rooted desire to do things for the young people of Texas. He was a man who had faith in what he was doing.

He received an uncalculated extra dividend from his work with the NYA. In doing that work, he built for himself a strong and lasting foundation of political strength.

It could hardly have been otherwise. Within a year after Johnson had assumed the post of State Administrator for the NYA, there were thousands of young Texans who called him "Lyn" and regarded him as personally responsible for their economic salvation. This was no mean asset for a man who liked people for themselves, to be sure, but who also was consciously on the lookout for the political main chance.

Early in 1937 the chance came. Representative James P. Buchanan of Johnson's Central Texas congressional district died. A special election was called to name his successor. It would be a "sudden death" election. No matter how many candidates entered, the one obtaining the largest number of votes would win; a majority of all votes cast was not necessary for victory.

Johnson resigned his NYA job to become a candidate for Buchanan's unfinished term. There were nine other candidates, several of them much better known than Johnson. They had more money for campaigning. They had the backing of the political conservatives, who were shying away from a continuation of New Deal policies. Newspaper comment at the time of Johnson's announcement of his candidacy revealed that he was not considered a serious contender.

The young candidate's platform was for the most part couched in exceedingly general terms. He said he stood for "a decent living" for every American citizen. He called for policies that would give farmers and ranchers equal opportunity with other occupational groups "for recovery and progress." He declared that he favored "the right of labor to have work" as well as "a sound national program to support and develop business."

That was all very well so far as it went. Johnson understood clearly that it did not go far enough to insure victory for him. What he had to do, he knew, was to dramatize his candidacy and get people to talking about him.

A short time before, Roosevelt had announced his plan to "pack" the Supreme Court. The proposal had aroused tremendous controversy, with most articulate Texans and organs of public opinion strongly opposed to it. Johnson added support of Roosevelt's Court plan to his New Deal platform.

In his opening speech at San Marcos, site of his college days, he delivered his challenge:

"support for
'packing'
court"

[35]

"If the people of this district are for bettering the lot of the common man; if the people of this district want to run their government rather than have a dollar man run it for them; if the people of this district want to support Roosevelt on his most vital issue, I want to be your congressman.

"But if the people of this district don't want to support Roosevelt, I'll be content to let some corporation lawyer or lobbyist represent them."

He shrewdly made it clear to the voters of the district that they were in the national spotlight, that the decision they were called upon to make was of the most solemn and far-reaching import.

"This," he pointed out, "is a local campaign for the election of a congressman in the heart of a Democratic state, a campaign of such importance and magnitude that the eyes of the nation are focused upon us. This national issue which you will vote on is commanding the keen attention of the people throughout the country."

The immediate result of this was one Johnson had foreseen. The other candidates, who had stated their opposition to the Court plan, turned their fire on him. With all of them talking about him, he was getting more publicity than any other candidate. With all of them declaring their conservatism in ever stronger terms, he was lining up virtually all of the hard-and-fast New Deal vote.

In addition to these advantages, he worked harder than anyone else. His rangy form turned up in towns and communities in all the ten counties of the Tenth

Congressional District. He was at his campaigning day and night. So was Lady Bird. So were all the energetic and enthusiastic young friends he had made during his work with the NYA—and their families and the friends of their families.

Throughout the district people were working to elect this young man to Congress simply because someone they knew had written them and asked their assistance. It was the kind of snowballing of support that was to serve Johnson well in every political race of his career.

Two days before the election, the candidate entered an Austin hospital for an emergency appendectomy. He was in his hospital bed when the returns came in the night of April 10, 1937.

He had almost twice as many votes as his nearest opponent.

The day after the election Johnson issued a statement in which he said: "I'm not going to get up and make a lot of speeches this first term. I don't believe I can set the world on fire and go up there and reform the United States of America right away."

· IV ·

The freshman started his congressional service with the warmth of Franklin D. Roosevelt's personal good will.

At the time of Johnson's success at the polls, the President happened to be on a cruise in the Gulf of Mexico off the Texas coast. He let it be known that he wanted to have a talk with this young man who had marched so successfully behind the New Deal banner in a state where there were rumblings of dissatisfaction among Democrats.

When the presidential craft docked at Galveston, Johnson was brought aboard and introduced to Roosevelt by his warm personal friend, Texas Governor James V. Allred. Roosevelt then invited Johnson to ride with him through Texas on the President's special train. On that trip Johnson told the President all about the kind of campaign he had waged. He managed, characteristically, to get in a few words about the importance of two big unfinished dam projects in his congressional district.

The Texan made no fight against succumbing to the famed Rooseveltian charm.

"He was a great man and you knew it five minutes after you first met him," Johnson told a friend afterward.

"He caused you to feel you wanted to do what he wanted you to do. And he had about the quickest mind of any man I've ever known. It was hard to keep up with him in conversation. He was always a jump or two ahead."

Johnson was making an impression of his own. Before he left the train, Roosevelt suggested that he might be "a good man to help out with naval matters" in Congress. The Navy was, of course, the President's prime darling and he was always on the lookout for opportunities of winning friends and influencing congressmen in its favor.

"Here's a telephone number," the President told the young congressman-elect near the end of their train ride together. "When you get to Washington, call it and ask for Tom. Tell him what we've talked about."

This "Tom" was Tom Corcoran, the famed and ebullient Tommy the Cork, who was such a great power in the early days of the New Deal. Once in Washington, Johnson wasted no time in getting in touch with him.

Johnson was sworn in as a member of Congress by Speaker William B. Bankhead on May 14, 1937. A few days later, as he stood in the rear of the House chamber, one of the great men of the House of Representatives, Fred Vinson of Kentucky, a member of the powerful House Ways and Means Committee, came up to him.

"Young man," the Kentuckian drawled, "I am indebted to you for a good dinner and an excellent conversation."

Johnson looked at him with surprise.

"I was invited to the White House for dinner," Vinson continued, "and the President was, as always, a most delightful host. I kept wondering just what it was he wanted from me. I knew it was something. Finally, he said casually—oh, very casually—, 'Fred, there's a fine young man just come to the House, and I think he would be a great help on Naval Affairs.' He meant the committee, you know."

As the two stood there, the "fine young man" still not fully understanding, the droning voice of the Clerk of the House announced the appointment of Johnson of Texas to the Naval Affairs Committee. It was an assignment of a kind not often given a new member. And it was only the first of many good turns done Johnson by his friend in the White House.

Grateful though he was to the President for his interest and firm as ever in his conviction that Roosevelt was truly a great man, the new congressman soon showed that he had no intention of acting as a rubber stamp of approval for Administration proposals. He had a mind of his own. He was not a man to be swayed from his convictions by personal charm, no matter how potent.

A few weeks after he assumed his seat, the House had up for consideration the President's veto of a bill to extend low interest rates on Federal farm land loans for another year. Sam Rayburn, who had been named House Majority Leader at the beginning of the session, took the floor to appeal that the veto be sustained. Johnson nevertheless voted to override.

It was not an easy thing to do, this going against the

wishes of both the President and Rayburn, his good friend and political godfather. But Johnson's reasoning was logical enough. He simply was convinced that the low interest rates were needed by farmers generally and by the farmers of his own district in particular.

The Tenth Congressional District of Texas was always first in his thoughts. He regarded himself as its servant, working in the House of Representatives to protect its interests. And, of course, as a matter of practical politics there was wisdom in doing everything for his district that he possibly could do.

As things turned out, he could do a great deal.

In his first two years in office, Johnson had the distinction of securing probably more Federal projects for his district than any other member of Congress was able to get.

His first efforts were directed at obtaining Federal financing for the multi-million-dollar Lower Colorado River Authority of Texas as a public works project. He was determined that cheap public power should be made available in connection with flood control and reclamation on the Colorado River.

The "power trust" was a favorite target of the New Deal. Johnson joined wholeheartedly in the fight against it. He was a fervent advocate of the program of the recently established Rural Electrification Administration.

"The farmer's income is low and some way must be worked out to bring it back to a normal and reasonable level," he argued. "While we are trying to do that, there is no reason why the farmer should not have electricity at cheap prices now. He needs it to help him with his work, make his home a better and more comfortable place to live, and to give him the opportunities available to city folks."

Congressman Johnson had not forgotten his boyhood days on the farm, where the family used kerosene for lighting, his mother did the laundry in zinc tubs and he and his brother pumped water by hand. "So far as electric power was concerned." he declared, "we were no better off than my grandfather had been when he lived on that same farm."

Announcement was made in January, 1939, that the Central Texas empire of public-owned electric utilities had become a reality with the execution of a contract for purchase by the Lower Colorado River Authority of properties owned by a private company in a sixteen-county area. Most of the area was included in Johnson's district.

There had been hard fights along the way. Once, at a meeting between Johnson and directors of the LCRA and officials of a private power company, the Congressman had flared up and told the utility president to go to hell. That ended the meeting.

Afterwards, the late Alvin J. Wirtz, general counsel of the Lower Colorado River Authority and a personal friend whose seasoned judgment Johnson deeply respected, asked the young firebrand to come by his office. Johnson expected that Wirtz wanted to do as the other LCRA directors had done, to shake his hand and congratulate him warmly on his fighting spirit. But that was not the older man's purpose.

"Listen, Lyndon," he said when the two were closeted in his office. "I've been around this business a long time. I know it must have made you feel good when those other fellows told you what a great man you are for advising the president of a big, powerful utility company to go to hell. But it broke up the meeting, you know. We still have to settle the issues we called the meeting to discuss.

"I learned one thing a long time ago, Lyndon," Wirtz added. "You can tell a man to go to hell easy enough—but he doesn't have to go."

good point

Johnson never forgot that lesson nor Alvin Wirtz either. Early in 1940 he was responsible for Wirtz' appointment as Under Secretary of the Interior, an office in which Wirtz served with the distinction that marked his entire career.

When Johnson first started pushing the plan to provide cheap electricity for farmers and other residents of Central Texas, Washington officials of the Rural Electrification Administration told him his program was too grandiose. "You want everything," they told him, "and all we can possibly do is think about giving you something."

Such words were a challenge to a man who looked for ways to do things rather than ways not to do them. He went ahead.

One result of his fight for extension of electric service to rural homes was the establishment in his own district

[43]

of the biggest rural electrification project in the world. Rates paid by farmers for electric power were slashed 25 per cent. Their use of electricity zoomed and the resulting benefits were plain.

Some of Johnson's own friends in Texas warned him, when he began his fight for rural electrification, that farmers could never be educated to use and pay for electricity. The Congressman replied with a standing offer of a Stetson hat to any person who could show him a rural electrification project where the farmers had not jumped at the chance to have electricity brought to their homes.

"I never lost a hat on REA!" was his proud boast.

A side result of his work in this field was an offer from Roosevelt of the job of REA Administrator for the nation. The President was well aware of the accomplishments of this protégé from Texas. Johnson declined with thanks, explaining he felt he had a contract with the people of his district to serve them in Congress and he aimed to live up to the contract. The offer, however, did nothing to lessen his growing prestige.

To the people of the Tenth District he was "the man who gets the job done." He threw his strength behind community efforts to obtain funds for new post office buildings for numerous towns. He worked for the establishment of Federal soil conservation projects in his district. He supported farm credit expansion and fought for lower freight rates for the Southwest. He continued to back such youth assistance projects as the NYA and the Civilian Conservation Corps.

One Christmastime some friends in Austin took him on a tour through a slum area of that state capital. Johnson was horrified to see the conditions in which the people of the area—mostly Negroes and Mexicans—were living. He went back to Washington determined to get something done about the matter, and he was able to persuade Congress to earmark half a million dollars for a public housing project in Texas.

He found that Negro farmers were often overlooked in the administration of the various New Deal efforts to put agriculture back on its feet. He went to work to correct the situation. Milo Perkins, assistant administrator of the Farm Securities Administration in the late 'thirties, said of Johnson, "He was the first man in Congress from the South ever to go to bat for the Negro farmer."

pushes aid to negro farmer

No proper request from an individual constituent was too trivial for Johnson to give it his personal attention. He laid down a rule for his staff that every letter received must be answered within twenty-four hours. When the work grew too heavy for the staff allowed his congressional office, he hired additional personnel and paid them from his own funds. He worked and his employees worked ten, twelve, fifteen hours a day.

"Lyndon was a real pusher," recalled a friend who watched Johnson's career from its beginning. "In those days he was maybe a little too cocky and sometimes he made people sore. He didn't develop his smoothness until later, but he did get things done.

"His gangling figure was everywhere on Capitol Hill.

He knew more members of Congress and more congressional secretaries than men who had been around Washington for years. He was a sharp trader and he knew how to get what he wanted. Even then, when he really turned on the charm it took a tough customer to stand up against him.

"People who knew Lyndon then were never surprised at his later successes. If there ever was a prototype of a young man going somewhere in politics, it was Lyndon Johnson during his first few years in Congress."

Johnson simply applied what he had learned as a congressional secretary about the mechanics of getting things done in Washington—and he was not without certain unusual advantages.

He had ready access to the White House. The President liked him and in addition Grace Tully, Roosevelt's personal secretary, took a great fancy to the Texan and made it easy for him to get the presidential ear. He could always count on Rayburn for assistance when it was needed. Wright Patman, another veteran Texas congressman who had served with Johnson's father in the Texas legislature, was also very helpful. Too, Johnson had become a prize pupil of Carl Vinson on the Naval Affairs Committee.

As war clouds broke over Europe and the United States began to look more closely to its own defenses, Johnson's position on that committee became increasingly important, his personal influence steadily more potent. He did more than any other one man to bring about the construction in Corpus Christi, Texas, of a tremendous naval air training base. It was his hand that guided the Administration in designating the Texas cities of Houston and Orange as sites for shipbuilding yards. He played an active part in the establishment of a Naval ROTC unit at the University of Texas and a Naval Reserve Station in Dallas.

These defense projects were not located in his congressional district. But in each case, Johnson considered, the city was a logical place for the particular activity set up there.

He was convinced that the United States would not be able to avoid becoming involved in the war. He knew the nation was far from ready, and he wanted to do anything he could to help it get ready. He was anxious for his own state to make every possible contribution.

Feeling this way about the immediate future, he was one who considered it essential that Roosevelt be nominated for an unprecedented third term as President.

Not all Texans agreed with him. In fact, there was strong sentiment in Texas for the nomination of the state's own John Nance Garner, the conservative rancher who was Vice-President during Roosevelt's first two terms. The Garner movement was an implicit threat to the unity of the Democratic Party in Texas.

Johnson admired and respected the Vice-President. Many of his own friends favored Garner for the nomination. But the congressman from the Tenth District felt that in the troubled year of 1940, as perhaps never before in the nation's history, a split among Democrats would be tragic.

He and Rayburn talked the matter over and then consulted with Roosevelt. After gaining his approval, they proceeded to work out an agreement with the Texan's backers that the state convention delegation would be instructed in favor of Garner for President—with the provision that the delegation would be pledged not to join any stop-Roosevelt movement.

Typically, Johnson remained on the best of terms with both sides of the potential controversy, averted by this agreement. He was one of the few men in the country who was trusted by the Garner people at the same time that he was a favorite of President Roosevelt.

The gentleman from Texas found work to do in the congressional campaigns of 1940. The Republicans needed to gain only forty-eight seats to capture control of the House of Representatives. A few weeks before the election, it looked very much as if they would get them.

The Democratic Congressional Campaign Committee was in a state of near-collapse. Activity had slowed down to such an extent that hard-pressed candidates over the country hardly bothered to ask the committee for help. Some of the people around committee headquarters were ready to throw in the towel.

Realistic and hardheaded Sam Rayburn (who had become Speaker of the House in September of that year, after William Bankhead's death) and Democratic Floor Leader John W. McCormack of Massachusetts went to Roosevelt and told him bluntly that something had to be done, and at once. The President asked for suggestions.

His staff had one ready. It was that Lyndon Johnson be put in charge of the campaign committee.

The next morning Johnson was in charge. He had a secluded office and no official title. His only instructions were to elect Democrats to Congress. He imparted his own enthusiasm and sense of urgency to an enlarged staff. He and the staff worked fifteen and eighteen hours daily during the remaining three weeks of the campaign.

The results spoke for themselves. The Democrats came out of the election stronger than ever. Instead of capturing the House, the Republicans actually lost six seats.

Johnson had been responsible for actively assisting more than 150 Democratic candidates for Congress. The successful candidates were not likely, considering the you-scratch-my-back-and-I'll-scratch-yours nature of the business of politics, to forget the help that had been given them.

As for his own re-election, there was no difficulty about that. He had been named to his first full term in Congress in 1938 without opposition. He was re-elected in 1940, again without an opponent.

As the "phony war" in Europe was succeeded by a terrifyingly unbroken string of Nazi victories, Johnson began a series of warnings to all who would listen that the United States was lagging behind in its preparedness program. His closeness to Roosevelt and other high figures in the Administration made him keenly aware of how far short the country was falling of the certain future need.

In an address before the Texas legislature in April, 1941, he earnestly challenged all elements in American life to join in subordinating every other consideration to accomplishing as rapidly as possible the gigantic task of getting ready for war.

He spoke with an eloquence unusual for him.

"How much time do we have to get ready?" he asked.

"The truth is," he answered, "we don't have any time.

"We don't know, in days, hours, weeks and months, when this hurricane may come to us. When we lose a minute wrangling among ourselves, we lose something that all the gold at Fort Knox, Kentucky, can't buy back. With every second wasted, we rush one step nearer universal disaster.

"I come to you today as a friend of American labor. But to labor I want to say this: When you vote to strike, you must think not only of your liberties but also of those superior liberties of every citizen of your country. You must think of your government and what it requires to save you and your precious rights.

"I have been the friend of business and industry. Still, there are privileges superior to yours and above those of any other minority in America. Your government can call on you and you are bound to respond when it must defend you and your precious advantages.

"I have fought a long battle for the farmers. But to farmers I say: Government can call on you, too, and you must answer.

"The security of the whole country is above that of any single group—labor, capital or farmer. When, in the scramble to save yourselves individually, all you minorities become willing to sacrifice the whole people for yourselves, you will jump the trap of your own gallows.

"We cannot be free men and, at the same time, disorganized men, bull-headed, obstinate, selfish men."

The joint session of the Texas legislature gave him an ovation.

The next day, back in Washington, Johnson called on Roosevelt at the White House a few moments before the President was to hold a press conference. The Texan emerged with an anouncement that he was a candidate for the unexpired term of Senator Morris Sheppard, who had died April 9. He read the announcement from the steps of the White House.

A few minutes later, at the President's news conference, Roosevelt was asked for comment on the Johnson announcement. He observed that there were three things to be said about the Texas senatorial contest.

"First," the President went on, "it is up to the people of Texas to elect the man they want as their Senator; second, everybody knows that I cannot enter a primary election; and third, to be truthful, all I can say is Lyndon Johnson is a very old, old friend of mine."

The President authorized direct quotation of his remarks.

Johnson's announcement of his candidacy was brief, referring to his experience in Washington and promising continued support of the President and his policies. In Texas, the announcement itself was overshadowed in the newspapers by the story of the "blessing" Roosevelt had bestowed upon the candidate.

This blessing was not unmixed in its effects. A hard core of opposition to the Administration had come to life in Texas. To those comprising this opposition—and there were powerful figures among them—Johnson was anathema by the very fact of Roosevelt's approval.

Other strong candidates were in the race for the Senate seat, among them Governor W. Lee O'Daniel, a self-styled "hillbilly" politician of extremely conservative views. Martin Dies, a former congressman and one-time head of the House Un-American Activities Committee, and Gerald C. Mann, the popular and able Attorney General of Texas, also were in the running.

O'Daniel and Dies were vitriolic in their denunciation of the New Deal and of Johnson as a New Deal pet. O'Daniel made a calculated appeal to the spirit of isolationism that had sprung up instinctively among many Texans as the war in Europe cast a growingly ominous shadow over the world.

Johnson set the tone of his own compaign in his opening speech. His theme then, and thereafter, was summed up in the warning, "It is later than we think!" He declared the country was in greater danger than it had been at any time since adoption of the Declaration of Independence. He called for Texans to stand with the President in the dangerous international crisis. He urged that the preparedness program be intensified. He advocated all-out aid to Britain.

Again and again he solemnly told his audiences. "I love peace. I hate war. And if the day ever comes when my vote must be cast to send your boy to war, that day Lyndon Johnson will leave his seat in Congress to go with him."

With respect to domestic issues, Johnson showed himself to be neither an extreme liberal nor a hidebound conservative. At a time when the middle of the road was far from being the most crowded place in the political world, that was where he stood.

on domestic issues

In his campaign speeches, he called for full parity prices for farm products; said he favored a nationwide system of old-age pensions, with payments starting to pensioners when they were sixty years old; advocated maternal and child care by the Federal government; staunchly upheld the doctrine of states' rights; declared that the government should prevent labor as well as capital from taking advantage of the national need in the present emergency.

As to the charge that he was a "yes man" for the Administration, he met it head on. Yes, he admitted, he was a yes man, a particular kind of yes man.

"I am a yes man for everything that is American," he said. "I am a yes man for anything that will aid in the defense of this Republic. I am a yes man to the Commander-in-Chief, as every good soldier should be in time of emergency."

Johnson was the first Texas candidate for political

office to make extensive use of the airplane in campaigning. He covered more ground and saw more people than any of his opponents. Adding to the hectic air of his campaign were the enthusiastic, if not always professionally expert, efforts of the thousands of young men and women who remembered how "Lyn" had helped them when he was State Director of the National Youth Administration. These loyal friends constituted the only organization he had.

Johnson's three principal opponents had statewide reputations. He was not at all well known outside the ten counties of his congressional district. He had started far behind. All through the later part of the furious campaign, public opinion polls showed him gaining strength at a rapid rate. On the eve of the election, the poll figures placed him barely ahead of the field, and this was another election in which a simple plurality of the votes cast meant victory.

Five hours after the voting ended on June 28, 1941, available returns from throughout the state showed Johnson leading O'Daniel by some three thousand votes. Gerald Mann was a fairly strong third and Martin Dies trailed. Numerous minor candidates received a sprinkling of votes.

On the second day after the voting, Johnson's lead over O'Daniel increased to five thousand votes. At that time 96 per cent of the ballots had been counted. Newspapers published detailed biographies of Johnson. Congratulatory messages poured in from all over Texas and from Washington.

But returns were still trickling in from small counties in far sections of the state. Johnson, who had devoted so much of his campaign to warnings that the nation must be prepared to meet the menace of Nazi aggression, received barely half as many votes in the ten leading German counties as O'Daniel polled. Here alone was the margin, and then some, by which the race was won.

German counties

Final returns showed O'Daniel was the winner by 1,311 votes out of a total of almost six hundred thousand cast.

Johnson's eager friends urged him to demand a recount. He refused. He was disappointed but not bitter.

"That's the ball game," he said. "Let's play again some other time."

He flew back to Washington to resume his duties in the House of Representatives.

Five months later the Japanese bombed Pearl Harbor. An hour after he had voted for the declaration of war, Johnson, for several years a member of the Naval Reserve, asked to be called up for active duty. Within three days he was a lieutenant commander in the Navy, the first member of the House of Representatives to go into uniform.

1st to war

· V ·

Johnson was on active duty in the Navy for only a little more than seven months. But he covered a great deal of territory before July, 1942, when President Roosevelt ordered all members of Congress who had been serving in the military forces back to their work in Washington.

After entering the Navy, he was placed on duty in San Francisco, attached to the office of the Chief of the United States-New Zealand Navy Command. He immediately started fretting to go overseas.

On a between-trains visit with his brother Sam Houston, who was then working in Denver, Johnson made it clear that he had enough of stateside duty.

"I'm not finding out anything about the war," he complained. "I'm not doing anything. I would be worth more to the country in Congress than I am in this assignment. I'm going to Washington and talk to the Boss. He's got to get something done about me."

He went to Washington and visited the White House. While he was in the city, he spent a little time in his own office in the Old House Office Building. Lady Bird was in charge there, having taken over as her husband's unpaid stand-in to keep the work of the office going. Johnson himself, immediately after going on active duty, had notified the House Sergeant-at-Arms that he would not accept his congressional salary while he was in the Navy. He drew a lieutenant commander's salary of $3,000 annually instead of a congressman's pay of $10,000 a year.

Shortly after returning to San Francisco from his Washington trip, Johnson was on his way to New Zealand. He was busy enough from then on.

By the time he was called back from active duty, he had ranged widely over the Pacific Area of Operations. Seeking information on which to base a report to the President, he had spent several months in Australia with General Douglas MacArthur. He had been on a patrol bomber which, after having a motor knocked out by Japanese fighters, barely managed to get back to its New Guinea home base.

MacArthur had personally bestowed on him the Silver Star for gallantry on this mission. Johnson had volunteered as an observer, stated MacArthur's citation, "to obtain personal knowledge of combat conditions . . . over hostile positions in New Guinea." In the face of enemy fire, "he evidenced marked coolness in spite of the hazard involved" and "his gallant action enabled him to obtain and return with valuable information."

He had survived the crash landing of a Flying Fortress in Australia. "God was with me all the way," he told his mother when he got back home.

A later report by one of the crew members of the crashed plane revealed that Johnson operated in the

Navy pretty much as he had in civilian life. The report appears in W. L. White's book, *Queens Die Proudly*, published in 1943. After describing the crash landing of the *Swoose* on an isolated Australian ranch, the crew member continued:

"We got out. Pretty soon Australian ranchers began crawling out of holes in the ground—I don't know where else they came from—and right away Lieutenant Commander Johnson gets busy. He begins to get acquainted.

"They tell him where we are and some of them go off to get a truck to take us into town where we can telephone, and more keep coming, and Johnson is shaking hands all around, and he comes back and tells us these are real folks—the best damn folks in the world, except maybe the folks in his own Texas.

"Pretty soon he knows all their first names, and they are telling him why there ought to be a high tariff on wool, and there is no question he swung that country for Johnson before he left. He was in his element. I know he sure swung the *Swoose* crew. He can carry that precinct any day."

The congressman had no trouble with his own precincts in the Tenth District of Texas during his absence, even though it was election year. In the spring of 1942, his name was filed as a candidate for re-election through petitions signed by more than twenty-two thousand qualified voters. In a letter to Lady Bird Johnson telling about the petitions, the organizers of the movement said, "It is the overwhelming sentiment of the voters that Lyndon B. Johnson should again be nominated for Congress."

Johnson, then in Australia, did not even learn he was a candidate until more than two weeks after the final date for filing his candidacy. Nobody came out against him.

As he resumed his seat in Congress, Johnson was gravely concerned about the war outlook in the Pacific area. Immediately after his return to Washington, he had a long session with Roosevelt and gave the President a frank, down-to-earth appraisal of the situation. He warned in speeches, on the floor of the House and elsewhere, that it was possible for the United States and her allies to lose the war.

In one of his first statements he took up the cudgel for the fighting men he had come to know in New Zealand, Australia and New Guinea, hitting out at the ineffectiveness of some of the high-ranking brass.

"We must get rid of the indecisive, stupid, selfish and incompetent among our generals, admirals and others in high military positions," he declared. "We must make it clear that it is no longer a crime to cut red tape.

"We are going to have to give our men leadership and equipment superior to that of any in the world. We are going to have to move quickly to coordinate dive bombers and domestic politics, tanks and military strategy, ships and the will of the people. Management and manpower are going to have to be closely woven into a smoothly functioning machine devoid of departmental squabbles and petty jealousies."

Representative Johnson was notably a man who had to have a crusade. He had one now that was very close to his heart. He sounded its theme again and again, as in a speech he delivered in the fall of 1942 on the occasion of the official scrapping of an old battleship, the *Oregon*.

"What about the scrapping that needs to be done elsewhere?" he demanded. "What about dollar-a-year men who make us wonder whether we hadn't better devalue the dollar a little further? What about overstaffed, overstuffed government that worries along like a centipede, too good in the production of legs and not good enough in the production of arms?

"While we have fighting to do abroad, we have scrapping to do at home. Scrapping of deadwood in thinking, of inefficiency in methods—yes, and of ineffectiveness in men, men who have become entrenched in power, men who love their country and would die for it, but not until their own dangerously outdated notions have caused others to die for it first.

"Today," he said caustically, "there are thirty-three Federal agencies working on the postwar situation—exclusive of Adolf Hitler's men, who are working on the same situation in case we don't win."

He blasted waste: in military manpower, in war plant worker absenteeism, in military procurement.

He was made chairman of a special investigating subcommittee of the Naval Affairs Committee. This group forced the Department of the Navy to adopt more businesslike methods of procurement. It brought about the rewriting of the Navy's contract for petroleum from the Elk Hills Field in California, an action which alone saved the Treasuury a small fortune.

His subcommittee labeled as "unjustified and inexcusable" the Navy's practice of staffing desk jobs in Washington with enlisted men who were qualified for sea duty. Johnson brought to light large-scale abuses and laxities in Navy requests for draft deferments for civilian personnel.

He spearheaded a drive in Congress to end absenteeism in war plants after the Naval Affairs Committee had drawn up a documented report showing that absenteeism cost the shipbuilding industry alone more than 16,700,000 man-hours in a single month, a loss of approximately 10 per cent of the industry's entire working force. Johnson introduced a bill requiring all naval contractors and subcontractors to make quarterly reports of unjustified absenteeism to draft boards.

He gave his support to the Smith-Connally Labor Disputes Act, which provided for a thirty-day waiting period before strikes could be called and prohibited jurisdictional strikes, boycotts and sympathy strikes. His backing of this legislation brought down on his head charges from some labor leaders that he had "sold out to the war profiteers."

Johnson had not lost his feeling for labor. He could understand and sympathize with the problems of industry in dealing with government in wartime. He realized that some waste of money and manpower was inevitable in the fast building up of a huge military establishment.

But, along with such understanding, he was determined that first consideration must be accorded the American men in combat with a deadly enemy, men like the crew of the plane on which he had been an official observer when it was hit by the Japanese in New Guinea.

"When I watched those boys fighting to keep that plane going, something was burned deep into me that I cannot forget," Johnson once said during this period. "When those boys and the others like them come back, I don't want to see the bitterness in their faces, the disillusionment in their eyes, which would come from the knowledge that there was something more I might have tried to do to help them—and didn't do it."

As the tide of the war began to turn, the Texan was thinking of what was to come after.

Specifically, he appealed for planning by community leaders and heads of industry everywhere to avoid the economic depression that was being predicted in some quarters for the postwar period. Months before the end of the war in Europe, he showed the trend of his thinking in a letter he sent to newspaper editors in his congressional district. He had some definite proposals to offer.

"I should like to see every school in my congressional district take inventory and plan such repairs, improvements and modernization as they feel essential," he told the editors. "I should like then for the city and county governments to do likewise. I am hopeful that someone will organize private industry and that when the armistice is signed industry will have plans well under way for the necessary conversion.

"A new world is going to open up to us."

He was also deeply concerned, as the end of the war neared, about the threat that the military machine the United States had constructed would be completely dismantled. He had been named by Rayburn as one of the members of a newly created House Committee on Postwar Military Policy. This group was charged with shaping security legislation and policies for the postwar period. Johnson later was appointed as one of the nine House members of the Joint Committee on Atomic Energy.

The war ended and there swept over the country an understandable but hardly realistic demand to "Bring the boys home!" without delay. Military hardware by the thousands of tons was simply junked overseas. Planes, tanks and guns were abandoned. Congressional pleaders for adequate military appropriations, for a system of universal military training, had hard going.

"We must keep strong!" Johnson said. "We must be strong militarily and productively and morally. We must have military strength to fulfill our moral obligations to the world.

"Our supreme duty today is to underwrite the future. We must have a strong police force to protect us from criminals, an Army and Navy strong enough to carry out our pledge to help the United Nations police the world."

The headlong rush of the American people away

from war and thoughts of war could not be checked. Even so, Johnson took the lead in fights to stop the premature closing down of the synthetic rubber industry, to check the sale at junkyard prices of war plants worth many millions of dollars and to bring about the establishment of a seventy-group Air Force in the face of strong opposition.

It was a time of confusion and unrest in Washington and the nation. People were realizing that the end of the war had not automatically solved all their problems.

Americans generally still felt much of the sense of loss that had gripped the country when Roosevelt died. Johnson's own feeling of this was deeply personal.

In an interview with William S. White of *The New York Times* on the day after FDR's death, Johnson had blurted out that the late President had been a "second daddy" to him. He had then recapitulated for White all that Roosevelt had done for him through the years since he came to Congress. He had reviewed the great humanitarian advances that had been made under Roosevelt's leadership.

Years later, in a brief formal statement in the Senate on January 30, 1956, seventy-fourth anniversary of Roosevelt's birth, Johnson once again restated his tremendous admiration for the New Deal President.

"We are still too close to the period which is inescapably associated with his name to have historical perspective," he said. "But even at this range, it is apparent to every American that he was one of the giants of all times.

"He was a controversial figure—but in the sense that all great men are controversial. He was a leader of courage and conviction, and such men live constantly in the swirling tides of national and international conflict.

"As one who was closely associated with our late President, I will never forget the meaning of his leadership to our country.

"He became President at a time when we were dispirited, discouraged, groping, almost with a sense of hopelessness, for a way out of our difficulties. He left us with a sense of courage and a feeling of buoyancy which will never desert us in our hours of trial.

"The verdict of history is still to be written. But however the book is finally closed, the last line must say that Franklin D. Roosevelt was a man capable of facing the terrible problems of terrible times."

That was his estimate of Roosevelt when time had eased the emotional shock of the President's death. Feeling as he did, Johnson nevertheless held steadfastly to his conviction that the country was bigger than any man, no matter how great. His attitude was shown in a comment to one of his secretaries a day or two after Roosevelt's death.

The secretary had said, half-weeping, "I feel so lost. Who is there now? Who is there for the country?"

"Why, honey," Johnson said quietly, "there's Truman."

His faith was strong that the country would continue to go forward. His strongest belief has always been in the American system, not in individual men.

In the difficult postwar period Truman was not able to retain for long the bipartisan support in Congress that was given him when he first succeeded to the presidency. The Republicans captured control of both houses of Congress in the 1946 elections. Even before that, many former New Deal Democrats had given aid to the Republicans in blocking various Truman proposals.

Johnson did not join in the sniping at the man in the White House. He was busy, physically and mentally. He was trying to do his job in Congress, but he was also giving sober thought to his own affairs and his personal future.

· VI ·

Many of Johnson's friends in Texas were taking it for granted that he would be a candidate for the United States Senate in 1948, the final year of W. Lee O'Daniel's term. Johnson himself was not so sure.

He would be forty years old in that year, with nearly a dozen years of service in the House of Representatives back of him. His position in his district was strong. He felt he probably could continue to be re-elected without a great deal of difficulty. But he wondered if he wanted to spend the years that would be necessary to give him enough seniority to attain a position of real leadership in the many-membered House.

As for the Senate seat, he was by no means certain in his mind that he could get it if he tried. He was never overconfident about such matters. Coke Stevenson, the popular wartime Governor of Texas, had announced his candidacy for the senatorial post. So had a forceful Houston lawyer named George Peddy. It was generally expected that O'Daniel would be a candidate for re-election.

Johnson thought about, and talked with his wife and a few intimate friends about, getting out of politics altogether.

He was restless. He and Lady Bird now had two little girls, one and four years old, and he wanted to be able to spend more time with his family. Also, he wanted to make money, which he knew he would never be able to do in politics.

A few years before, Lady Bird had bought a radio station in Austin and turned it into a paying proposition. Johnson felt that, with the inhibitions of his official position removed to give him a free hand in promoting the station, he could help in its continued development. He was thinking about a television station, too. He wanted to get in on the material possibilities of the new world he had predicted was going to open up once the war was finished.

In May, 1948, he went down to Austin prepared to make an announcement that he would not offer himself as a candidate for the Senate.

"I got down there," he related later, "and called in a few of my close friends and told them what I planned to do. There wasn't much talk about it, no display of disappointment on their part. They seemed to accept my decision.

"Then about four o'clock in the afternoon a group of young men came to see me. I had known some of them since the NYA days. They had helped me in my 1941 race for the Senate. Some of them were making good records of their own in public service.

"They told me I had been the cause of their taking an interest in public affairs and working for better government. They said that gave me a certain obligation toward them. They asked me, quietly and without any argument, to change my mind about the Senate race."

It was hard for him to reconsider his decision. His busy mind was already planning ahead for the private life to which he proposed to return. But he did reconsider and announced his candidacy that evening at a hastily called press conference.

This was not to be a special election, such as the one that had sent Johnson to Congress in 1937 and such as the one he had come so close to winning when he ran for the Senate in 1941. This time he was a candidate in the Democratic primary in July. If no candidate obtained a majority of all votes cast, there would be a runoff one month later between the two top men. The winner of the second primary would become the official Democratic nominee and could be expected to have only token opposition from the Republican Party in the general election.

If Johnson lost, he would not be able to return to his House seat as he had done in 1941. This time, he was either going to be elected Senator or be out of public office.

O'Daniel surprised most observers by declining to stand for re-election. But Coke Stevenson was a formidable opponent. A homespun conservative rancher and longtime politician, he had a good record as Governor, an office from which he had retired at the beginning of 1947. Before that he had been Lieutenant Governor and Speaker of the Texas House of Representatives. He had no political machine as such, but he could call on

[69]

many powerful friends for help. His standing was high with the everyday citizens of Texas. A statewide poll of public opinion near the end of his tenure of Governor showed that 71 per cent of the people approved of his administration.

Johnson had no readymade organization, but he had the raw material for one. Thousands of former NYAers in every part of the state were ready to turn out in an effort to do what they had failed to accomplish in 1941. Many important Texans were indebted to Johnson for help he had given them in dealing with Washington officials during the war years. He had comparative youth. He was thirty-nine. Stevenson was sixty.

In his opening speech in Austin on May 22, Johnson based his campaign on "three bold signposts on the road we should travel toward a better tomorrow." These signposts he listed as Peace—Preparedness—Progress.

He called for the establishment of a governmental climate that would favor the maintenance of a strong industrial system. He declared the United States must have the world's most powerful Air Force and an Army and a Navy adequate to any task. He said continued scientific development, including research into peacetime application of atomic energy, should be fostered by the Federal government.

On the subject of what the United States could do to help insure a peaceful world, Johnson suggested:

"We can strengthen the United Nations.

"We can keep open the free channels of trade.

"We can stand up to the warmakers and say, This

far and no farther—as we did in Greece and Turkey.

"We can help free men with the Marshall Plan.

"We can tell the world about America and American aims."

There was nothing wrong with this program, of course, but experienced political observers among Johnson's friends warned him that it was not calculated to set the voters on fire. He must, they agreed, find an issue.

The campaign was off to a rather dull start. Stevenson was traveling around over Texas by automobile, stopping in small towns to shake hands with people on the streets and making speeches over a radio network. The ex-Governor paid no attention to his opponents, contenting himself with calling attention to his own public record and to the need for economy in the Federal government. Peddy, the Houston lawyer, also was delivering competent but uninspired attacks on Federal extravagance and bureaucracy.

Shortly after his opening campaign talk, Johnson captured the news headlines momentarily by coming down with a kidney infection and being dramatically flown by his friend, the famed Jacqueline Cochran, to the Mayo Clinic in Rochester, Minnesota, for treatment. He was there for two weeks.

He came back to Texas with an inspiration. A week later he was up in the air in a helicopter equipped with a public address system and dubbed by him the "Johnson City Windmill."

In the weeks that followed he leapfrogged all over the

[71]

big state, coming down in towns and cities to make brief addresses to the people attracted by the helicopter and hovering over crossroad settlements and remote hamlets to blast down the information that he was Lyndon Johnson of Johnson City and was a candidate for the United States Senate.

the gimmick

At that time most people had never seen a helicopter. In many smaller settlements of Texas, most people had never seen a candidate for the Senate either. The opportunity to see both at once was not one to be missed.

It was a new political gimmick and was highly successful in getting listeners for the candidate's remarks about his program of peace, preparedness and progress. On his first day in the helicopter Johnson estimated that he saw and was seen by six thousand people. The flying windmill enabled him to present his candidacy to as many as fifty or sixty thousand individuals in a single week.

His campaign was off the ground, so to speak, but he still had not found the issue he wanted. It was presented to him not on a silver platter but on a workingman's spade near the end of June, when over a month still remained before the first primary.

the issue

State officials of the American Federation of Labor, holding a political caucus in Fort Worth, endorsed the candidacy of Coke Stevenson for Senator. The endorsement broke a precedent of fifty years' standing.

The former Governor had never been known especially as "a friend of labor." Surprise was expressed among political observers that the conservative Stevenson should get the nod from organized labor over Lyndon Johnson, considered by many Texans to symbolize what they thought of as the dangerously radical theories of the old New Deal and the new Fair Deal.

But Johnson had voted in Congress for the Taft-Hartley Act. This law, passed over Truman's veto in 1947 with the aid of most of the Democrats from the South, was designed to eliminate the abuses of powers granted organized labor under the Wagner Act. The Taft-Hartley Act set up certain protections for employers as well as employees, placed limits on the closed shop, regulated and restricted political contributions from union funds, and increased the burden of union responsibility in contracts between labor and management.

The general public regarded the act as a necessary curb on the tremendous power and influence the labor unions had come to possess. The law was popular in Texas. But leaders of organized labor bitterly stigmatized Taft-Hartley as reactionary legislation. They had vowed vengeance on those favoring its passage in Congress.

Johnson, who may have hoped that his whole record as a congressman would be considered by the labor leaders and would influence them at least to keep hands off the senatorial contest, leaped into the press with the charge that Coke Stevenson had made "a secret deal" with the unions. He appealed to Texans to write Stevenson and ask him how he stood on the Taft-Hartley Act.

"If my opponent has promised to repeal the law, the

people have a right to know," Johnson declared. "If he has not made such a promise, the people have a right to know.

"Also," he added, "I think the laboring men should ask their leaders to tell them openly why they wanted the unions to break a fifty-year precedent and endorse a faltering candidate who did not have the courage to sign or veto the state's vicious anti-labor law when he was Governor."

Johnson had his issue. He never let it go.

From that time not a day passed without his issuing a demand for Stevenson to state his stand on Taft-Hartley. Perhaps there were many people in Texas who had no knowledge at all of the law's provisions. Probably there were many who did not care. Nevertheless, Johnson's persistent, dramatic, accusatory cry—"How does he stand on Taft-Hartley? Why won't he tell you?"—had its effect.

It was not enough, however, to give Johnson the nomination in the first primary or even to place him in the lead. He received 405,617 votes to Stevenson's 477,077. Nine other candidates, with George Peddy the only serious contender, received a combined total of 320,000 votes. There had to be a runoff.

A week after the election Johnson was back in full cry. He abandoned his helicopter, announcing that it was too slow for him, and flew from one city to another to go after votes. Stevenson had led in almost all the metropolitan counties, and Johnson saw his only hope lay in whittling down his opponent's lead in those areas.

He had his campaign organization working around the clock. Lights in the big house in Austin which served as campaign headquarters burned all night.

Johnson attacked his opponent's record as Governor and charged him with being isolationist in his approach to foreign policy. He pointed out that his own record in the House of Representatives was one of steadily increasing responsibility and that his experience fitted him for service in the Senate. He reviewed his votes in Congress to show that he was not an extremist of either the left or the right.

Most of all, day after day, he hammered at the Taft-Hartley issue.

"How does my opponent stand on Taft-Hartley? Why won't he tell you? Is he ashamed? Is he afraid? What kind of deal has he made with the big labor leaders?"

Johnson lost so much weight that the flesh of his face seemed to have melted away. Chronic sleeplessness had driven his eyes far back into his head. Sometimes his voice was a croak. He never stopped going.

A Stevenson adherent, reviewing the campaign long afterward, said, "Our big trouble was that we had a candidate who really preferred to say nothing and an opponent who was determined to say something and keep saying it. And what he said hurt."

It was one of the toughest political campaigns Texans had ever witnessed. It had a melodramatic finish.

The runoff brought Johnson 494,191 votes and Stevenson 494,104 votes, a difference of eighty-seven votes in Johnson's favor.

Stevenson announced that he would not accept the result as valid. Suits and countersuits were filed in county, state and Federal courts simultaneously. Johnson eventually won all along the line.

He had to be officially certified as the Senate nominee by the Democratic State Executive Committee. The committee was as closely divided as the voting populace. But Johnson was certified by a vote of twenty-nine to twenty-eight.

Texas Republicans came to life and anounced that the Democratic nominee would receive more than token opposition this time. Jack Porter, a Houston oilman who had left the Democratic Party in the early forties, carried the Republican banner in the general election. Porter was a vigorous and knowing campaigner. He later became Republican National Committeeman from Texas during the Eisenhower Administration. And he fought hard. He enlisted the aid of Coke Stevenson, who took to the radio to urge his followers to support Porter.

Johnson, who did no more campaigning, won by a two-to-one vote in the general election.

He was headed for the Senate at last, forty years and a few months after his grandfather had predicted it would happen.

· VII ·

When Lyndon Johnson took his seat as United States Senator from Texas in January, 1949, he had been considerably sobered by the close, bitter campaign and its Hairbreadth Harry finish. He was hurt by jeering references to him as "Landslide Lyndon." But he was realistic.

"Almost exactly one-half the people who voted in the Democratic primary didn't want me for their Senator," Johnson told friends. "My big job is to get them to change their minds about me."

The best way to do that, he reasoned, was to work hard in the Senate for all the people of Texas, those who had opposed him as well as those who had supported him.

He deliberately set out to do the kind of things for the state that he had done for the Tenth Congressional District. He assembled around him a considerably enlarged staff, the core of which were a few persons who had been with him through most of his career as a public official. He interested himself in every problem affecting Texas. He threw his tremendous energy into making his office a service office for all Texans. This was something he knew how to do.

In the Senate, he adhered to the tradition that freshmen members should be more seen than heard. He received the committee appointment he wanted and for which his experience in the House best fitted him, being named to the Senate Armed Services Committee. He studied the history of the Senate and its methods of operation. He studied the characteristics of individual Senators.

Several old friends with whom he had served in the House of Representatives were now in the Senate. He made new friends—men like Richard B. Russell of Georgia, Edwin C. Johnson of Colorado, Ernest McFarland of Arizona and Virgil Chapman of Kentucky. The scholarly and able Russell, who had become chairman of the Armed Services Committee, was particularly impressed with the energy and alertness of his new committee member, and the two men became fast friends.

Very early in his Senate term, Johnson began building up a team of expert advisers. He maintained his close relationship with Sam Rayburn, who was again Speaker of the House following the Democratic victory of 1948. The new Senator from Texas constantly soaked up knowledge from such sage and experienced counselors as Rayburn, Russell, his old friend Chief Justice Fred Vinson, Stuart Symington, Justice Tom Clark, and many others.

During working hours and social hours, Johnson was hard and heavy at his self-imposed task of learning to become the most effective Senator he could possibly be. He and Lady Bird never went in very extensively for the social life of Washington. Even when Johnson did

[78]

attend parties, he was usually to be found off in one corner of the room talking politics.

"All my life," Johnson has said, "when I have been faced with a particular problem, I have tried to find the man who knew more than anybody else about that problem. Then I have asked for his advice. After I get the best advice available to me, I try to follow it."

During his first year in the Senate, he became increasingly concerned about the place of the United States in a world where victory in the fighting war had been succeeded by a dangerous cold war between onetime allies. Adequate preparedness was always a cause close to Johnson's heart. He now set out to buck the trend toward letting the American defense system go to pot.

The United States' initial monopoly of atomic weapons had not lasted long. Communism had spread over once-free European countries and had sealed the back entrance to Soviet Russia through the conquest of China. It seemed to Johnson, looking with alarm at these facts, that Communism had achieved most of its major goals everywhere except in the United States and the nations allied with the United States by means of the Atlantic Pact.

In Johnson's view, the American military establishment had been whittled down to a dangerously low point. After the President and the Budget Director decided in 1948 to impound funds that had been appropriated to keep aircraft production plants tooled up and productive, Congress refused to force the issue.

The fight for a seventy-group Air Force had been

lost. The Air Force would have been torn to shreds except for the persistent efforts of Johnson and Stuart Symington, Assistant Secretary of War for Air before the military services were merged and first Secretary of the Air Force in the new Department of Defense. The two men, fighting hard, did all they could. Neither of them considered it was enough.

Economy in defense was the watchword in the Executive Department. From his work on the Armed Services Committee, Johnson knew that only a small percentage of even the reduced defense budget was earmarked for the vital purpose of research and development of new weapons. He knew, too, that the services were racked by intramural jealousies in spite of the Unification Act that had brought them all together under the Department of Defense. Successive reductions in strength had been made not only in the Air Force but also in the Army and Navy.

The situation seemed most alarming to Johnson, considering the troubled state of the world. He called for a searching review of American foreign and military policy.

On February 28, 1950, he made one of his most important speeches. It was delivered before a meeting of the American Association of School Administrators in Atlantic City. Its subject was "Our National Security."

It this address, after presenting some of the facts about the cold war which was constantly threatening to become hot, Johnson accorded consideration to the charge that there was "fat" in the nation's defense system and to the assurance of the economizers that they wanted only "to cut fat, not muscle."

"There is fat in the defense establishment—physical fat and mental fat," Johnson conceded.

"I am most anxious that we fry out the mental fat," he declared, and continued:

"I believe the time is near when the proper authorities must determine the facts concerning the strength of our military establishment. This should be done not in a spirit of bias or a spirit of petty revenge, but in the hope of making full use of this nation's scientific and technological resources.

"In addition, I think we should look into our stock-piling program so that we can avoid the great hazard of being caught short in essential strategic materials.

"Also, we must look thoroughly into the condition of our military housing and other factors relating to personnel so that the morale of our forces will not be lowered and their efficiency reduced at this period when the utmost is demanded from all of us, individually and as a team.

"We have the advantage of a long history of free public education, which has given us the world's greatest reservoir of enlightened manpower. We have the further advantage of freedom, which permits the full use of the minds and learning of our citizens.

"That is our great source of strength. We must put that strength to use in the military as in all other areas of our government.

"For five years, we Americans perhaps have to some

extent isolated ourselves behind the security of an atomic monopoly. We were tired from the exertion of war, weary of crisis. We concentrated our national energy and our national talent on our own comfort more than on our security.

"This is true in the formulation of our foreign policy, true in the formulation of our domestic policies, and true of the broad conduct of our military establishment.

"That isolation is ended.

"We can no longer indulge laziness or sluggishness.

"We must challenge ourselves—and in that challenge we shall find the salvation of the world.

"The facts are grim, but we must face them. By facing facts squarely we can and will find the answers to our problem of survival.

"This is not the darkest hour in our national history. If the challenge of the moment stirs our imagination and our capacity for invention, we may see the brightest hour of civilization.

"There is hope for us and for the world—so long as we keep hope alive."

This address in Atlantic City attracted national attention and helped pave the way for the position Johnson was rapidly to assume as the conscience of the Senate on matters pertaining to the national security.

Four months after he spoke, the Communists of North Korea marched southward and President Truman ordered the armed forces of the United States to the defense of South Korea.

Johnson hailed the President's action as necessary and

praiseworthy. It was an action, he said, that "gives a new and noble meaning to freedom, gives purpose to our national resolve and determination, and affirms convincingly America's capacity for world leadership."

In the days that followed, his compelling voice was heard increasingly often in the Senate chamber.

He pointed out that the forces of the United Nations were seriously outnumbered.

He declared that American military equipment available for the task in Korea "is plainly inadequate in quantity, and it is not the right kind."

He called attention to the two-edged fact that the problem of supply in South Korea was overwhelming and that prospects for correcting the situation were bleak.

"We must not," he said in a Senate speech, "act too slowly, too cautiously, with too much consideration for the comfort of those who remain behind.

"We can no longer sit by and see our strength decimated by delay—defeat—retreat."

He urged three immediate steps: development of a long-range global plan of strategy; immediate full mobilization of available manpower; prompt mobilization of the American economy.

He also called for an end to blaming the Administration for the conflict in Korea. "The Communists, not President Truman, were responsible for the invasion of South Korea," he reminded. "The quicker we direct our hostility to the enemy instead of our leaders, the quicker we will get the job done."

In the latter part of July, 1950, Johnson introduced a resolution, which the Senate promptly passed, establishing the Preparedness Investigating Subcommittee of the Senate Armed Services Committee. He was designated chairman of the subcommittee and was off on a two-year series of investigations that strengthened the military establishment in a crucial period and at the same time saved American taxpayers several billion dollars.

The subcommittee was in effect a successor to the National Defense Investigating Committee headed by Harry Truman in 1941 when he was a member of the Senate. That committee had been a powerful watchdog during the war and actually was Truman's springboard to the vice-presidency and eventually to the presidency.

Members of the new subcommittee promptly called on Truman at the White House to enlist his support of the effort they planned and to get the benefit of his experience with a similar panel. Truman welcomed them cordially and told them he would see that they had the complete cooperation of the Executive Department. He called Johnson back for a private word at the end of the conference.

"The most important single thing to remember," he advised, "is to make sure that you have the support of the minority members of your committee. To be effective, this committee must work in a completely bipartisan, or nonpartisan, atmosphere."

Members of the subcommittee, along with Johnson, were three other Democrats, Estes Kefauver of Tennessee, Virgil Chapman of Kentucky and Lester Hunt of

FDR and Johnson were first brought together (1937) by Texas Gov. James V. Allred in Galveston. (*Jack Miller*)

Lieutenant Commander Johnson at General Mac-Arthur's wartime headquarters in Australia.

Called back from the Navy by the President, Johnson visi wartime plants like the Orange, Texas, shipyard. (*T. L. Gun*

Johnson used a helicopter to cover Texas in his 1948 campaign for the U. S. Senate.

Johnson and his wife show his mother the sights of Capitol Hill.

At the start of the 1949 session of Congress, Senator Arthur Vandenberg of Michigan, President Pro Tem of the Senate, administered the oath of office to four freshmen: Frear of Delaware, Johnson of Texas, Douglas of Illinois and Kerr of Oklahoma.
(Wide World Photos, Inc.)

On duty with NATO in 1951, General Eisenhower came to Washington to appear before a joint meeting of the Senate Armed Services and Foreign Relations Committees.

Truman calls for "Peace with Freedom." Speaking at a buffet of the Democratic National Committee, Truman said he would accept only "peace with freedom and justice" from the Communists. Left to right, seated: Vice President Alben Barkley; Truman; House Speaker Sam Rayburn, Texas; Senate Majority Leader Ernest McFarland, Arizona. Standing: William Boyle, Chairman of National Committee; Sen. Lyndon Johnson; Sen. Clinton Anderson, N. M.; Rep. John McCormack, Mass.; Rep. Percy Priest, Tenn. (*United Press*)

(The Saturday Evening Post)

Johnson has been known to have as many as four telephone calls working at once.

Senators Margaret Chase Smith, Leverett Saltonstall and Johnson,
all members of the Senate Armed Services Committee, watch a
television screening of the first hydrogen bomb test.

(Jimmie Willis)

Johnson and Supreme Court Justice Tom Clark, fellow-Texan and longtime friend.

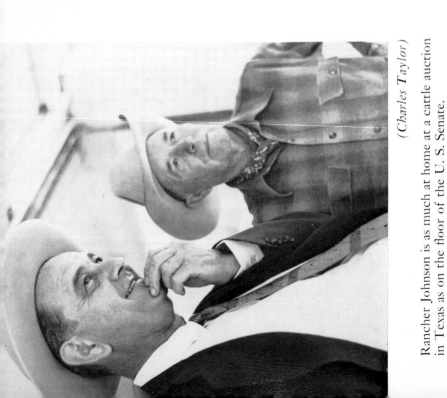

(Charles Taylor)

Rancher Johnson is as much at home at a cattle auction in Texas as on the floor of the U. S. Senate.

Not long before his death, Senator Robert A. Taft wrote Johnson: "I do not see how any Majority and Minority Leaders could cooperate better than we have done, and it is due largely to your thoughtfulness and consideration and good judgment."

Campaigner Johnson and voters. *(Neal Douglas)*

Churchillian quips know no party line. (Rep. Joe Martin of Massachusetts at left of Churchill, Chief Justice Earl Warren in center, Johnson at immediate right of Eisenhower, Knowland next to Eisenhower.)

Stuart Symington of Missouri and Richard B. Russell of Georgia are members with Johnson of the Senate Armed Services Committee. *(Reni Photos)*

Four candid shots of a face rarely in repose.

Two former First Ladies—Mrs. Woodrow Wilson and Mrs. Harry Truman—were among honor guests at the Washington Jefferson-Jackson Day Dinner of 1955.

Heart to heart in the spring of 1955.

(United Press Photo)

Johnson in 1954 became the youngest Majority Leader in Senate history. Sam Rayburn, another Texan, has served longer than any other man as Speaker of the House.

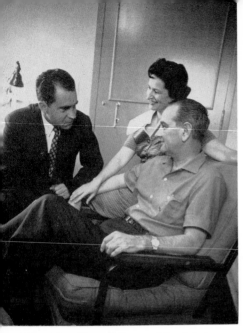

Vice President Nixon visited Johnson (and Lady Bird) at Bethesda Naval Hospital as the Senator convalesced from his 1955 heart attack. (Courtesy *Life* Magazine © *Time* Inc.)

Senator and Mrs. Johnson alighting from the plane that took them to Texas after the Senator's recovery from the heart attack. (*Wide World Photos, Inc.*)

After his heart attack Johnson learned a hard lesson: how to relax. (*San Antonio Express*)

TV's Arthur Godfrey takes a thermometer reading of the heated
swimming pool on Johnson's Texas ranch. *(Radio Post)*

Senator Stuart Symington visited Johnson on the LBJ Ranch in
Texas in the summer of 1955.

LBJ Quints—Lady Bird and Lucy Baines, Lyndon B. and Lynda Bird, Little Beagle Johnson. "We're a one-suitcase family," says Johnson of their common initials.

Johnson's first birthday after his heart attack was a happy one.

(San Antonio Express)

Mother and wife join in looking over congratulatory messages the Senator received on his forty-seventh birthday—August 25, 1955.

The Johnson home on the banks of the Pedernales River in the Hill Country of Central Texas. *(San Antonio Express)*

Speaker of the House Sam Rayburn and Adlai Stevenson were visitors at the LBJ Ranch in the fall of 1955.

Senator Bob Kerr of Oklahoma and Johnson are longtime cronies.

Grace Tully, personal secretary to FDR for many years, is now executive assistant to the Majority Leader of the Senate.

Estes Kefauver admires the Democratic mascot sent Johnson by a Texas friend.

Wyoming; and three Republicans, Styles Bridges of New Hampshire, Wayne Morse of Oregon and Leverett Saltonstall of Massachusetts.

It would have been difficult, even in such a haven of individualists as the United States Senate, to find a more diverse group. Yet this committee, made up of seven strong personalities with widely varying political philosophies, issued forty-four reports (many of them on highly controversial subjects) during its existence and every report was unanimous. Lyndon Johnson had learned a great deal about the art of getting along with people and bringing them to agreement.

At the organization meeting of the Preparedness Investigating Subcommittee, the chairman set four guideposts of conduct.

1. The members pledged themselves against mere headline hunting. They promised to develop the substantial, not to exploit the sensational.

2. They pledged themselves to nonpartisanship, with politics "left outside the door to the committee room."

3. They pledged themselves to avoid second-guessing battlefront strategy. They conceived of their job as being not one of telling the generals and admirals how to fight the battles but rather one of making sure that the military leaders and the men fighting under them had what they needed to win those battles.

4. They promised to be frank, impartial and straightforward in all their inquiries and recommendations.

These were high standards. They were adhered to rigidly. The basic rule Johnson laid down for the committee was to be "blunt but not unfair, zealous but not persecuting, helpful but not uncompromising."

"Our big job," he told his fellow-committeemen, "is to get the defense effort away from hardening of the arteries of imagination and ingenuity."

The new panel started off right by obtaining the services of an outstanding attorney as general counsel. He was Donald C. Cook, who had served as chief counsel to the old House Naval Affairs Committee's defense probe which Johnson had headed. When he was called on to work with the new committee, he was vice-chairman of the Securities and Exchange Commission. Later he was elevated to the chairmanship of the SEC. At Johnson's request, he worked without pay and on a part-time basis—nights and week-ends, mostly—as the Preparedness Investigating Subcommittee's general counsel and chief braintruster. His brilliant performance was a factor of tremendous importance in the success of the subcommittee.

Johnson and Cook assembled a staff of investigators and got at the job before them.

That job consisted of two major undertakings. One was to conduct an overall manpower study, seeking to determine the nation's capabilities for raising a large armed force without crippling agriculture and industry. The other was to see that the industrial mobilization program authorized by Congress was carried out expeditiously and without waste in order to provide guns, tanks and other equipment for men called into service.

The panel's first investigation dealt with the nation's

synthetic rubber production program. The development of the synthetic rubber industry had been vastly important during the war. But after the war ended the industry had deteriorated badly, with some of the rubber plants being sold to surplus dealers and dismantled. The country was coming dangerously close to rubber shortages and the cost of natural rubber was rising constantly.

The report of the subcommittee's findings blasted the Munitions Board for slowing down instead of speeding up rubber stockpiling. That report also contained some barbed observations on the failure of the agency to cooperate with subcommittee investigators. The Munitions Board had let three weeks pass without even bothering to reply to urgent inquiries from the subcommittee.

"Either the Munitions Board has a program or it has not," the report stated. "If it has a program, it could readily be described. If it has no program, it should be candidly admitted.

"In any event, if the diligence with which the Munitions Board addressed itself to our inquiry is any measure of the manner in which it attends to its other duties, its competence would seem to leave something to be desired."

This forthright initial report of the new subcommittee had three immediate results.

Munitions Board Chairman Hubert B. Howard abruptly resigned.

The National Securities Resources Board accepted the subcommittee's recommendations that sales of rubber plants as surplus property be stopped at once, that all available rubber plants be put back into full production as rapidly as possible, and that notice be served on the world that the United States would not buy natural rubber at exorbitant prices but instead would increase domestic facilities for synthetic rubber production. The recommendations were formulated into a program adopted by the Executive Branch. Resultant savings to American taxpayers were estimated at more than a billion dollars.

The third effect of the report was to place the Preparedness Investigating Subcommitte and its chairman in front-page newspaper stories all over the country.

The United Nations forces, composed largely of Americans, were being beaten in Korea. The American people at home were disturbed and angry about the course the fighting had taken. Here came a member of the United States Senate who agreed with them, who voiced their own feelings about Federal bureaucracy that hindered the fighting men instead of helping them, who proved the existence of conditions which they had suspected.

The people understood and applauded language like this, used in one of Johnson's early reports: "Many officials who have carved an empire for themselves out of the Washington jungle are reluctant to surrender any part of their domain. The eventual loser is the taxpayer. He finds himself paying two men to do the work of one or, what is even worse, paying two men to do jobs that should not exist at all."

Johnson had announced that the subcommittee would not seek headlines. It had no need to seek them. The information its investigators uncovered and the sharp, relentless quizzing of witnesses by the chairman in public hearings was the natural stuff of which headlines are made.

But the headlines were only the outward evidence of the group's activities. More important was the fact that its work got the right kind of results.

A subcommittee report disclosed that price gouging by tin producers was skyrocketing the cost of the defense program. Corrective action saved an estimated half a billion dollars in public funds.

Another investigation uncovered waste of critical manpower due to Air Force "hoarding" of available men. After the report came out, the Air Force took steps to induct its men in an orderly manner to prevent a repetition of the excessive crowding at various fields.

In the Army, Johnson found staff sergeants issuing golf equipment, expert pilots acting as post exchange officers, trained tank mechanics recalled to Reserve units that had no tanks. As a result of the subcommittee's pinpointing of such waste in a number of installations, the Army Chief of Staff decided he could squeeze out two additional combat divisions without increasing the size of the Army.

Two reports discussed the substandard housing available to dependents of military personnel, forced by economic circumstances to live in packing crates, mule sheds, tool sheds, and in one case a "house" built of whiskey bottles and old tin cans. The military launched a program to make more adequate housing available.

Another report disclosed illegal gambling activities near a large Air Force base, with servicemen being victimized on a wholesale basis by slot machines and other devices. Local authorities clamped down on these activities after the report was made public.

Down in Johnson's own state of Texas, committee investigators found a farmer had bought $1,200,000 worth of surplus airplane parts for $6.89 and then sold them back to the government for $63,000. No illegal action was involved. It was, in Johnson's words, simply an "astounding case of shortsightedness." It bore out his charge that, even after the development of the Korean crisis, Defense Department officials approved the sale as "surplus" of everything from aircraft engines to war industry plants. The policy was changed after the Preparedness Investigating Subcommittee started bearing down.

Sometimes the high brass at the Pentagon complained about the subcommittee's activities. On the whole, however, Johnson found the military services willing to accept recommendations based on findings of fact and to correct deficiencies. The subcommittee earned respect by its thoroughness, its fairness, its strict adherence to the purpose for which it was established.

Often a mere hint of action would cause a bad situation to be corrected. For example, the Secretary of the Air Force once suddenly canceled a $1,650,000 order for white dress gloves for officers because he had heard that Johnson was thinking about—just thinking about—making an investigation of gloves in the Air Force.

From a financial point of view, the Preparedness Investigating Subcommittee was an excellent investment for the government. Savings of tax funds as a result of its work were variously estimated at from three to more than five billion dollars. The total cost in committee payroll and operating expenses was less than $275,000 for the entire time the subcommittee functioned—from July, 1950, to February, 1953.

It was a record which Johnson viewed with understandable satisfaction.

During this period, as chairman of the subcommittee and on the floor of the Senate, Johnson continued to wage his unremitting battle against what he termed "a siesta psychology" with respect to the world situation in general and the Korean conflict in particular.

In a speech in December, 1950, after the Chinese had entered the battle on the Korean peninsula, he declared that in the six costly months since the beginning of hostilities the government's planning and action had continued to be on a basis of "day to day and hour to hour."

"We have committed ourselves only to a policy of not committing ourselves," he charged. "What is the result?

"For the common defense we have thrown up a chicken-wire fence, not a wall of armed might."

He got to his feet behind his desk in the Senate to pose a solemn question: "Is this our last hour?

"Is this the hour of our nation's twilight, the last fading hour of light before an endless night shall envelop us and all the western world?

"That is a question which we still have in our power to answer.

"If we delay longer, we can expect nothing but darkness and defeat and desolation.

"If we answer the challenge with courage and confidence and with the ability of which we are capable, we can, I am sure, triumph over our foes."

During these blackest hours of the war in Korea—the "police action," as it was officially designated—Johnson warned firmly that compromise and timidity, vacillation and expediency could result only in defeat, dishonor and destruction.

As a United States Senator, he called insistently for a national will to win.

As chairman of the Preparedness Investigating Subcommittee, he helped clear the way to victory by fighting against waste and for full utilization of the nation's manpower and industrial might.

During these years Lyndon Johnson did work of tremendous value to the United States, and became known to many thousands of Americans who had never before heard of him. And, of even greater importance, he gained the lasting respect and friendship of some of the most powerful members of the Senate.

· VIII ·

During the time he was earning for himself a position of growing prominence on the national scene, the Senator from Texas also was doing a highly specialized kind of job in the Senate for the Democratic Party. At the beginning of the 1951 session of Congress, Democratic members of the Senate unanimously elected Johnson as Majority Whip.

The position of Party Whip in the Senate is an important and taxing one. The Whip's principal responsibility is to see to it that members of his party are on hand to vote when the time comes for voting. Senators have many duties in addition to those they perform in the Senate chamber. Often, as the moment approaches for voting on a legislative measure, the Senators have to be located and notified that their presence is required on the floor.

The Party Whip needs to be a young, energetic, well-liked man. The youth and energy are necessary because of the physical demands of the job. The Whip must remain alertly at his post, no matter how far into the night the Senate may stay in session, and must be prepared to do a large amount of simple legwork. The popularity is a prime requisite because Senators may not at times relish being told they must drop whatever they are doing and go to the Senate floor for a vote.

Johnson met all three qualifications. He turned in an outstanding performance as Democratic Whip at a time when the Truman Administration was losing support among its members in Congress as well as among the American people generally.

One thing the job did for him was to put him in daily close contact with the most important men on the Democratic side of the Senate chamber.

In addition to getting members to the floor for votes the Whip's duties include staying constantly in touch with the Party Leader and acting in his place when necessary. At the time Johnson was named Whip Ernest McFarland of Arizona was elected Majority Leader. He was a man with whom the Texan could work smoothly and effectively. Both men occupied a middle-of-the-road position on party issues. Both were moderates. Both had persuasive personalities.

In assuming his new post, Johnson automatically became a member of the Democratic Steering Committee and the Democratic Policy Committee of the Senate. The function of the Steering Committee is to make party assignments to standing Senate commmittees. The Policy Committee, as its name indicates, sets party policy on important issues arising in the Senate.

In addition to McFarland and Johnson, the Policy Committee's membership consisted of Russell, Chapman, Theodore Francis Green of Rhode Island, Lister

Hill of Alabama, Brien McMahon of Connecticut, Joseph C. O'Mahoney of Wyoming, and Robert Kerr of Oklahoma. All these men except Kerr, who also had entered the Senate in 1949, were Johnson's seniors in service as well as in years. There was much he could learn from them.

"Skeeter" Johnston, present Secretary of the Senate and at that time Secretary to the Senate Majority, told an interviewer a few years later that he had the greatest admiration for the way in which Johnson conducted himself as Whip.

Johnston, whose experience as a Senate employee goes back to 1929, recalled that the Texan was generally looked upon by his fellow-Senators as a "comer."

"That's a good thing, of course, but it can be dangerous," Johnston said, speaking out of his wealth of knowledge regarding the Senate as an institution. "After all, Senator Johnson was just beginning his third year of Senate service when he was named Whip. That was moving along pretty fast. Some of the men he worked with every day had been in the Senate five or six times as long as he had.

"He felt his way very carefully. He didn't try to push himself forward too much. He deferred, as was completely proper, to the Majority Leader. But he was always there when he was needed. And even then he had a genius for getting along with people and causing them to get along with one another."

This was a period of growth and development for Johnson. Although the two houses of Congress are constitutionally equal, there is a tremendous difference between being one of 435 Representatives and one of ninety-six Senators. And Johnson was not merely another of the ninety-six. He was close to the top party leadership in the Senate.

Ever since he came to the House of Representatives he had been something of a crusader. Now, as a Senator, he still fought hard and determinedly for causes in which he believed. But he was changing. He was developing a potent ability to persuade men who differed violently to sit down with him in an effort to lessen somewhat the extent of their disagreements.

This training Johnson received during his service as Majority Whip was invaluable to him. He gained much; but he also contributed much and the worth of his contribution did not go unrecognized.

"The Senate will not soon know, and the country may never know," said Vice President Alben W. Barkley at the end of the 1952 session of Congress, "how the Senator has worked behind the scenes in ironing out differences between the Senate and the House and among Senators."

Barkley, who before becoming Vice-President had himself served as Senate Democratic Leader for a dozen years, expressed the considered opinion that Johnson had attained "a reputation and a standing never exceeded in the same length of time by any other member of the United States Senate."

The Vice-President was joined in his praise of the Majority Whip by Herbert A. Lehman of New York, a liberal whose views were often far removed from those held by Johnson. Lehman warmly congratulated Johnson as well as McFarland on "the spirit of unity" which had been achieved under their leadership.

Clearly, Johnson's star was rising in the Democratic Party. But the fortunes of the party itself were distinctly on the downgrade.

The Democratic Party had a heavy load to carry as it prepared for the general election of 1952. It was the year when appeals were made to clean up "that mess in Washington," the year of "the great crusade" on behalf of General Dwight Eisenhower. There was never a day during the campaign when the Democrats were not on the defensive.

Johnson supported Dick Russell in the Georgian's bid for the Democratic nomination for President. But after Governor Adlai Stevenson of Illinois was nominated, Johnson promptly announced that he would support the nominee.

Considering the times, considering the issues and personalities involved, considering above all that Texas was the state represented by Johnson in the Senate, it was a courageous decision.

In spite of Texas' position as traditionally an "in the bag" Democratic state, most of the state's leading newspapers had endorsed Eisenhower. Allan Shivers, who had been nominated by a heavy majority in the Democratic primary for another term as Governor, was urging Eisenhower's election. So was Price Daniel, the Democratic nominee for the Senate seat being vacated

1952 Campaign

[97]

by Tom Connally. Many of Johnson's leading personal supporters favored Eisenhower.

Heavy pressure was put on Johnson by some of his longtime friends. They urged him, since he would not support the Republican candidate, at least not to campaign actively for the Democratic candidate. If he felt he must vote for Stevenson, they counseled, let him do so without unduly advertising the fact.

Political observers whose judgment Johnson trusted assured him that the state probably would go for Eisenhower. He himself would be up for re-election in a couple of years, they reminded him. Wisdom dictated that he spend his time building up his own political fences instead of deliberately placing himself on what was almost certain to be the losing side in the presidential contest.

Johnson listened to his friends as always but he was not swayed by them.

"I just can't do what you are asking," he told one highly influential man, who had given him valuable support in both his unsuccessful and his successful races for the Senate. "It wouldn't be right, and I don't even think it would be smart. I believe the Democratic Party is best for Texas and the South and the nation. It's a firm conviction with me and I can't go against my convictions."

He lost that man as a supporter and he lost his personal friendship as well. He regretted the double loss and was deeply pained when word reached him that the man was castigating him as an ingrate. But there was no doubt in his mind about the course he should follow.

The regularly constituted State Democratic organization was backing Eisenhower. Rayburn set up a special Stevenson-Sparkman campaign committee with headquarters in Dallas. Many prominent Democratic officeholders conspicuously stayed away from the Speaker. Johnson was not among them. He and Rayburn worked together perhaps more closely than ever before during that fall of 1952.

"Lyndon did everything I ever asked him to do during the campaign," Rayburn said afterward.

Johnson made a number of barnstorming speeches on behalf of the Democratic ticket. In one three-day period he delivered more than twenty addresses.

When Adlai Stevenson made a tour of Texas, Johnson introduced him on his first appearance and then accompanied the Democratic candidate throughout the state on a special campaign train.

He gave the introductory address when Vice-President Barkley came to Austin to urge Texans to stay in the Democratic ranks.

Johnson also broadcast over a statewide radio network a carefully reasoned explanation of why he was supporting, as he proclaimed, "the entire Democratic ticket."

He said there were two major issues in the campaign: "prosperity for our people" and "peace for our world." He charged that the Republicans wanted the American people to ignore those issues.

"I won't ignore them," he declared.

He went ahead to describe, in down-to-earth language, the two issues as they appeared to him. It was a strong address by a man who believed wholeheartedly what he was saying, and was doggedly determined to say it regardless of whether the immediate consequences were beneficial or harmful to him.

After the election, in which Texas joined the nation in giving a majority to Eisenhower, Johnson contented himself with stating simply, "We have a new leader. I won't discuss the wisdom of the choice, but he is our leader. Some people have gone off into the corner to pout. Others want to tear down, but any jackass can kick down a barn. It takes a good carpenter to build a barn. We aim to build."

Out in Arizona, Senate Democratic Leader McFarland had gone down in defeat. When the Democratic Senators—reduced, even though just barely, to the minority—met in their first-of-the-session conference in Washington in January of 1953, Johnson was unanimously elected Minority Leader.

At forty-four, he was the youngest man ever to be named Floor Leader of the Senate by either major party. All hands among the country's political observers agreed he had his work cut out for him.

· IX ·

Not a few politically wise ones predicted that Johnson, as Senate Minority Leader in the Eighty-third Congress, would simply be administering a receivership in political bankruptcy.

They had reasonable grounds for such a belief. The Democratic Party was disorganized, in debt and without effectual leadership. A deep schism had long existed between the Southern and Northern wings of the party. Recriminations over the manner in which the losing national campaign had been waged were still being hurled back and forth.

Will Rogers once said, "I am not a member of any organized political party. I am a Democrat." The words never seemed more applicable than at the beginning of the year 1953. The experts peered into their crystal balls and saw ahead two more years of wrangling, with the North and the South fighting for control of the defeated party.

Johnson's election to the Minority Leadership, unanimous though the vote was, had nevertheless lacked the wholehearted support of perhaps one-third of the Democrats in the Senate. Johnson himself was well aware that members of the "liberal bloc" viewed him with apprehension. He recognized and at times commented wryly on the circumstance that too many people in Texas considered him little better than a Communist and too many people in Washington were firmly convinced that he was a Dixiecrat.

The Texan did not deceive himself about the difficulties that lay ahead. Just the same, he had no intention at all of acting as a referee in bankruptcy for the Democratic Party.

Eisenhower's sweeping victory had not been fully shared by Republican candidates for Congress. At the beginning of the first session of the Eighty-third, the Senate was composed of forty-eight Republicans, one Independent (Wayne Morse of Oregon, who announced that he was breaking away from the Republican Party but would vote with the Republicans to organize the Senate) and forty-seven Democrats.

This near equality in numbers could not, however, be accepted at face value. The range of differences among the Democrats in opinion on and approach to national issues was great. No one, except perhaps Lyndon Johnson, had much hope that there would be many occasions on which the forty-seven would act and vote as a unified whole.

Some of the muttering liberals among the Democrats felt their worst fears were confirmed when Johnson immediately made it clear that, so far as he was concerned, there would be no Democratic opposition to Administration proposals merely for the sake of opposition. He strongly disagreed with the sentiment often expressed in the past by Senator Robert A. Taft, Majority Leader of the Senate in the new Congress, that the "business of the opposition is to oppose."

Not so, said Johnson. In his view, "The role of a minority party is to hammer out a program that will solve the problems of America—not just to obstruct the work of the majority party."

"All of us," he reminded his colleagues and the country, "are Americans before we are members of any political organization. As the Senate minority, we Democrats will place the national interest above partisan considerations. When we are forced by our convictions to oppose Administration proposals, our opposition will be based on principle and will be expressed in a principled manner."

He elaborated on his concept of the proper role of a political minority in an address delivered early in the year at the Jefferson-Jackson Day Dinner in New York City. He attempted no "give 'em hell" pyrotechnics. His appeal was to the thinking mind, not to the emotional viscera.

"There are two courses open to a minority party," he told the New York Democrats. "It can indulge in the politics of partisanship, or it can remain true to the politics of responsibility.

"The first course is tempting to the weak, but ultimately would be rejected by the American people. The second course is difficult, but is the road upon which we can offer leadership to the American people that will be accepted.

"Our dedication must be to the politics of responsibility—to a statesmanship which is based upon the realization that we cannot survive unless our country survives.

"No course will be successful unless that thought becomes our guiding star."

Among Senate Democrats, meanwhile, Johnson was striving to gain acceptance of the thought expressed in one of the homely sayings he remembered his father often using: "In adversity the family draws closer together." Standing squarely between the left and right wings of his party, he understood them both. He used this understanding to get them together and keep them together.

He started off by demonstrating forcibly that, with all due respect to tradition, he was not afraid to depart from the beaten path in Senate procedure. Important committee assignments customarily were made on the basis of seniority. But Johnson was able, when he made the assignments at the beginning of the session, to persuade some of the Democratic elders to give up their claims to choice committee spots. That left the way open for giving good places to the freshman Senators who had won in 1952 in spite of the party's national defeat.

A few of the elders protested. Johnson told them a story drawn from his Texas boyhood. A lad he knew, Johnson said, on being denied a visit to a nearby city, complained bitterly that his brother had "been two-wheres and I ain't been nowheres." Johnson added that he could not see the logic of placing senior Senators two-wheres or even threewheres on important committees while capable freshmen languished at the bottom of the totem pole.

Every Democratic Senator wound up with at least one desirable committee appointment. With perhaps one or two exceptions, everybody was pleased. The new members were especially happy, of course, and that was important to the success of Johnson's plan to get Democrats to get along together, because some of these Senators were among the liberals who had not been overly enthusiastic about his election as Floor Leader.

Before long, even the old hands who had complained slightly about Johnson's departure from tradition were acclaiming the wisdom of his policy on committee assignments. Moreover, as they worked together under Johnson's adroit direction, the conservatives learned with some surprise that few liberal Senators came equipped with horns and a built-in gleam of wildness in their eyes. And the liberals found that there was more of wisdom than they had thought in some parts of the conservative philosophy.

The situation caused one deep-dyed conservative Senator to grumble good-naturedly to Johnson regarding one of the militant young liberals, "Lyndon, I'll never understand how in the world you got me to liking him so much."

The Democrats, who had been at odds with one

another so long, discovered the benefits of cooperative endeavor. They began to look for issues on which they could agree instead of searching for issues on which they were certain to disagree.

At the same time that the Minority Leader was meeting with such success in inculcating a spirit of unity into his followers, the members of the majority on the other side of the aisle dividing the Senate chamber were having their troubles with disunity.

Early in the first session of the Eighty-third Congress, it became evident that many Republicans in Congress were unwilling or unable to depart from their instinctive attitude of opposition to proposals emanating from the Executive Branch of the government. The fact that the new occupant of the White House was a Republican seemed to make no difference to them. They had long ago become accustomed to saying "Yes" when the President said "No" and to saying "No" when the President said "Please." It was hard for them to change.

The result was that a somewhat unusual form of bipartisanship came into being. It consisted, on some basically important issues, of a combination made up of the President, some elements in his own party and a majority of Democrats *against* a sizable and vociferous group of Republicans.

That was the case when Eisenhower asked for a renewal of government reorganization powers vested in the Executive, when he submitted to Congress a resolution condemning Communist bad faith with respect to international agreements, when he urged extension of the Reciprocal Trade Agreement Act, when he sent the Administration's Mutual Security bill to Congress.

In supporting the Administration on these and other matters, Johnson proved conclusively that his talk about "politics of responsibility" meant just what it said.

"The President must wonder at times," he commented sardonically, "whether he could not do a better job for his country if he were not weighed down by the Republican Party." Over in the House of Representatives, Rayburn, back at the post of Minority Leader, observed, "The present Administration needs more nonpartisan help than any administration we have ever had."

When Johnson and Rayburn could conscientiously give such help, they did so. When they found themselves opposed to Administration proposals, they did not hesitate to express their opposition in the most effective way available to them.

In steering the course of the Senate Democrats, Johnson proceeded by a set of carefully formulated rules. Basic among them was a policy of complete flexibility to permit each issue to be judged solely on its merits rather than its political origin. Along with that went a strict avoidance of personalities and name-calling. His third rule called for ready Democratic cooperation on any issue involving the national security.

These rules worked. They enabled Johnson to build up a Democratic record based on his "politics of responsibility" philosophy, while simultaneously giving the Democrats the heady experience of working together effectively instead of flying apart in all directions when they came up against a controversial question.

With a man as popular as Eisenhower in the White House, this was obviously sound political strategy. But it was more than that. It was an expression in action, not words, of the Minority Leader's conviction that the American people were not best served by extreme partisanship in government.

Naturally, he was not always in agreement with the President's proposals. The man who had refused to be a rubber stamp for a Chief Executive of his own party could not be expected blindly to approve every suggestion or request of a Republican President.

He resisted the Administration's efforts to cut down the strength of the Air Force, an old and often-fought battle for him. He opposed Administration-sponsored reductions in the work of the Soil Conservation Service. He castigated a plan to give the Secretary of Agriculture unlimited authority to reorganize his department.

Whether in opposition to the President or in agreement with him, Johnson was able to carry most of the Senate Democrats along with him.

His greatest strength as Minority Leader was the effectiveness of his personal work with individual Senators. He indulged in no tirades on the Senate floor. He never attempted to bulldoze, either publicly or privately, those who disagreed with him. He never questioned another Senator's motives, no matter how strongly he might doubt the soundness of his judgment. Above all else, he devoted himself for many hours a day to apply-

ing all that he had learned through the years about bringing men together in their thinking.

His friend, Dick Russell, gave a candid and realistic
summation of Johnson's assets at this period: "He
doesn't have the best mind on the Democratic side of
the Senate; he isn't the best orator; he isn't the best par-
liamentarian. But he's the best combination of all those
qualities."

As for the Republican Senators, he was on excellent
personal terms with most of them. They liked him and
Johnson always responded instantly to friendliness. He
and Majority Leader Taft, partisan foes though they
were, regarded each other with genuine regard and
friendship.

There was a special significance to this friendship.
Outwardly, two men could hardly have been more different. Johnson was gregarious, sentimental, persuasive,
all fire and energy. Taft, on the other hand, was often
withdrawn and often tactless, proceeding with his business, as William S. White wrote in his perceptive book
about the Ohioan, "in the flat uncaring manner of a man
driving a nail into a board." White correctly pointed out
that Taft wholly lacked the gift for people in the mass
that Johnson possessed in such abundance.

Yet the two men not only got along well in perform-
ing their official duties but enjoyed a warm personal
relationship as well. This was born after they assumed
the Senate leadership of their respective parties. Prior to
that time they had not really known each other at all.

Each approached the other warily during the early

days of the 1953 session, but the feeling-out period did not last long. They came to be closer than perhaps any other two members of the Senate. Johnson, Bill White reported in the book about Taft, "was one of the few men who could persistently heckle Taft, as he often did with soft mutters across the three feet of aisle space that separated their desks in the Senate, and not be glared down."

Their mutual regard had its genesis, no doubt, in the respect each felt toward the other as a man. Neither ever entertained the slightest doubt about the other's integrity. Both literally loved the Senate. Each valued a worthy opponent, and neither of them had any use for the kind of aimless, time-wasting chitchat that Johnson jeered at as "just visiting" and Taft forthrightly scorned as "nonsense."

It was necessary for the Majority Leader and the Minority Leader to work together if the Senate's business was to function properly. In the case of Taft and Johnson, both found the association a pleasure as well as a duty.

When Taft's tragic death came in the summer of 1953, Johnson stood up in the Senate with tears in his eyes to say, choking over the words, "No more honorable man has ever sat as a Senate leader for any party. I have lost one of the best friends I ever had."

During all this time, while he was working with the Democrats who composed his Senate constituency, Johnson never neglected his constituents in Texas. It was all very well to be Floor Leader and ex-officio chairman of the Senate Democratic Policy Committee. But he knew the people back home who wrote him four or five hundred letters a day, most of them containing requests that he do something or other, were mainly interested in his work for them as their representative in the United States Senate.

He filled their requests when he could. When he could not, he explained why and if possible offered a substitute service. He saw that all the letters were answered promptly.

He kept a stream of news flowing out of his office to the Washington representatives of Texas newspapers. He sent a "newsletter" regularly to the several hundred weekly newspapers in his state. He recorded a weekly radio "Report to the People" for use by Texas stations.

In the Senate, he supported and at times initiated legislation to provide assistance for drought-stricken areas, to improve the cotton acreage allotment system, to provide rural telephones as part of the Rural Electrification Administration's program, to aid military personnel and ex-servicemen, to authorize Federal assistance in solving Texas' long-range water supply problem.

He felt he knew pretty well what Texans generally needed in the way of legislation. He labored incessantly to get it for them. His rapid rise in the Democratic Party had not lessened one iota his determination to be the best Senator Texas ever had.

He was working harder than ever before in his life. At times he conducted his business on the run—literally. One afternoon, a staff member recalled, he and the Senator left the Senate Office Building to go over to the other side of the Capitol to record a radio broadcast. Johnson's car was parked only a few feet from the door of the building. But he actually sprinted that short distance.

"Lyndon," his wife complained, "acts like there's never going to be a tomorrow."

A typical day in the life of the Minority Leader was described at the time in a story written by Elizabeth Carpenter, Washington correspondent for several Texas newspapers. She wrote:

"Johnson's day begins at 6 when he starts reading the Washington morning newspaper and the *Congressional Record* which is delivered to his door. He shaves, bathes and calls his office to check on developments with the early staff, which has the mail open and the work under way. He usually talks to a Senator or two before breakfast.

"He breakfasts, and the car which is assigned to the Senate Democratic Leader picks him up at exactly ten minutes to 9. The driver has *The New York Times* for him daily, and he reads it on the way to work.

"Arriving at the office shortly before 9:30, Johnson confers briefly with the heads of his office staff. Then he starts receiving Texas callers. From 9:30 until 11:45 he talks to all the visiting Texans who want to see him. Then he rushes to the Senate chamber. . . .

"Sometimes he can sneak off for lunch, but other times he doesn't get to eat. He likes to have lunch served in his Capitol office when it's possible so he can dine with a group of Democratic Senators. Johnson can't put up with wasted time. So if he's worried about a farm problem he will invite to lunch Senators Russell, Allen J. Ellender of Louisiana and Clinton P. Anderson of New Mexico, all agricultural experts. If it's housing he may eat with Senators Burnet Maybank of South Carolina and Paul Douglas of Illinois. If it's budget or finance, he may have Senator Harry F. Byrd of Virginia or Walter George of Georgia. A defense problem means Senators Russell and Stuart Symington of Missouri. . . .

"Secretaries bring mail over to the Senate for Johnson to read and dictate replies. Texans who went to see him and missed him in the morning are brought over. He does a lot of conferring in cloakrooms with other Senators of both parties because he is convinced that no Minority Leader can be successful unless he has the respect and confidence of the majority party, too.

"The Senate usually stays in session until 6. When it ends, he heads back for the office. There he dictates more mail, reads Texas newspapers, returns telephone calls which have piled up during the day, checks with assistants on the progress they have made on assignments he gave them in the morning and talks with a few Senators. Often he goes back over to the Capitol to talk with Sam Rayburn before going home. These sessions explain the close teamwork between the Democratic Party in the two houses.

"It is at least 8 when he heads home. There he eats and falls into bed to read the evening newspapers and some of the papers he has brought home. He usually doesn't get up until morning—going to sleep when he finishes reading."

The pace was a grinding one day after day.

In the closing hours of the first session of the Eighty-third Congress, Johnson received what was to him a most acceptable reward for his efforts as a number of Senators reviewed his seven months of leadership.

It was started by Albert Gore of Tennessee, with whom Johnson had served in the House of Representatives. Gore was one of the freshman Senators who had profited by the leader's policy of giving desirable committee assignments to new members, and the Tennesseean expressed his gratitude. Then he said of Johnson:

"A strong party man, nevertheless he can and does place patriotism ahead of partisanship. His ability and his standards of integrity are, in my opinion, largely responsible for his phenomenal success as a party leader. Furthermore, as a Senator of his own party, I can testify that he has been a unifying factor unequaled since I have known the United States Senate. I think it is fair to say that at the beginning of this session the Democrats in the Senate were divided; but we end this session united."

Gore, one of the youngest men in the Senate, was succeeded on the floor by Green of Rhode Island, the oldest. Green also mentioned the tender, loving care Johnson had accorded young Senators and added, "I am grateful for the consideration he has shown to the older Senators and the idiosyncrasy which he has evidenced of himself being capable of understanding, rather than of misunderstanding. Both old and young have followed him gladly."

Mike Mansfield of Montana, another of Johnson's former House colleagues and also a new member of the Senate, declared that after eleven years of service in Congress he now felt for the first year "that I am a member of a unified party."

"As a Democrat," said Georgia's Russell, "I am proud of the record he has made. As an American, that pride is doubled."

Lister Hill of Alabama joined in: "Time and time again on this floor during this session we have seen our leader demonstrate his exceptional ability, his courage and, most of all, his devotion to our country and its welfare."

Lehman of New York, acknowledging the existence of "certain differences of opinion" among Democrats, stated that, nevertheless, "the area of agreement we have reached today is far greater than the area of difference."

"I do not believe," said youthful John F. Kennedy of Massachusetts, "any man ever took over a more difficult assignment than did Lyndon Johnson the first of this year. If the Democratic Party today stands united, and once more is asserting its voice throughout the land, I think that is due to no other person."

Even some Republicans spoke up about Johnson's "cooperation" and "nonpartisanship," among them William F. Knowland of California, who had succeeded Taft as Majority Leader.

At one time three Senators—Stuart Symington of

Missouri, Edwin C. Johnson of Colorado and the courtly Clyde R. Hoey of North Carolina—were on their feet seeking recognition from the presiding officer in order that they could participate in the outpouring of encomiums. They and others stressed repeatedly the harmony which now prevailed among Democrats, thanks to the leadership of the man from Texas.

It is not unusual, of course, for Senators to speak highly of other members of "The Club." Every so often something causes the Senate to break out in a rash of tributes to some individual, living or dead. But on this occasion, in the view of some longtime observers of the senatorial scene, the sentiments expressed went beyond the call of dutiful courtesy. There was a general feeling that Johnson had fully earned the plaudits he received.

Events of the session had borne out the statement of a writer for *Time Magazine* that "Lyndon Johnson is, for the Democrats, exactly the right man in the right place at the right time."

· X ·

Viewed with cold objectivity, Johnson's personal political status at the end of the 1953 session of Congress did not appear to be as demonstrably favorable as his standing among Senate Democrats. And he would be up for re-election in 1954.

Only the year before he had campaigned vigorously for a presidential candidate who had been turned down by a majority of the voters of Texas. Since then, no matter how much he had cooperated with the new Administration on certain issues, he had been the very active leader of the Senate opposition.

Besides, no one could say with certainty how much of the bitter feeling engendered by the 1948 senatorial campaign remained alive in the minds of those who had opposed him. Johnson himself remembered all too clearly the prediction of a Federal judge, during court proceedings following his squeak-through victory in the Democratic primary, that the man finally winning the Senate seat, whether it was Johnson or Coke Stevenson, would be a one-term Senator.

He knew, however, that he had worked hard at his job. He had done a great many things for the people of

Texas since 1943. He knew also that he had won over as loyal supporters some of those who had fought him hard in that year. He had kept his statewide campaign organization alive and vigorous.

Weighing all these factors, he felt he stood a good chance of being named to a second term. But it was not something he proposed to take for granted. Within a few hours after the adjournment of Congress he was on an airplane bound for Texas.

He had one simple purpose in mind: to see and talk with as many Texans as he possibly could during the remaining five months of the year.

He remembered the advice a seasoned colleague had given him when he first entered Congress. "The best way to keep your job," the oldster had told him, "is to use your franking privilege in Washington and your heel leather when you're back home." So Johnson embarked on a hard-driving "grass roots and heel leather" tour of Texas.

He let it be known through the press that he was available and invitations flooded him: to make speeches, attend barbecues, be honor guest at luncheon club meetings, open county fairs, ride horseback in parades, dedicate public buildings, appear before school assemblies. He accepted as many of the invitations as he could.

Talking to a newspaper reporter soon after his arrival in Texas, Johnson said he was trying to follow what a wise man had once told him were three good rules in politics: Do right; make yourself available; tell about your product.

[118]

"I am trying to report to the folks here at home about what Congress has been doing, especially what the Senate has been doing," he said. "I want them to know Lyndon Johnson, so that when I ask them for their votes they won't be likely to say they elect me and then never hear of me again. I want them to ask me questions about their problems, and naturally I want to do everything a Senator can do to help them."

He cut a wide swath over Texas, covering every part of the state and making well over two hundred talks to every kind of audience imaginable. The talks were labeled "nonpolitical" and, strictly speaking, they were; but Johnson did not neglect to tell about the product he was promoting.

One of his Washington staff members, who had never before seen Johnson in action among the voters, was amazed by the performance of his boss in this role. He found out that Johnson was as popular with "the folks" as he was with Senators.

"Why, he's a hero to the people down there," he later reported to some of his co-workers on Capitol Hill. "We would hit some little town and the Senator would be out on the street almost before the car stopped rolling. He'd start down the sidewalk, shaking hands, and pretty soon he would have quite a crowd following him—kids asking for his autograph, nice old ladies telling him what a fine boy he was, farmers grabbing him by the arm and saying they knew he would look out for their interests. I never saw anything like it."

In his formal talks, he discussed America's foreign

policy and the farm problem; told how the Democrats in Congress had aided the President on many occasions; expressed his enduring belief in the future of the nation; and emphasized the importance of working for peace from a position of strength.

By the time he returned to Washington in January, many leading Texas newspapers were saying editorially that Johnson should be returned to the Senate for another term without opposition.

He was not quite that fortunate, for Dudley Dougherty, a wealthy young oil man with views that were conservative even for a rich young Texan, announced as a candidate for the Democratic nomination for Senator. Johnson stayed on his job in Washington and never once took official notice of his opponent.

In the Democratic primary of July, 1954, he won the nomination by a vote of nearly three to one. It was a result that gave him deep personal satisfaction as he contrasted it with the narrow and controversial margin by which he had attained the nomination in 1948.

In the Senate, meanwhile, Johnson had continued to follow the pattern set during his first year as Minority Leader. With Joe McCarthy on the rampage, the Republicans were more divided than ever. The McCarthy political philosophy was far removed, of course, from Johnson's own views. He was strategist enough to take advantage of the uproar the Wisconsin Senator constantly created among members of his own party.

The Republican differences gave Johnson the opportunity to underline the fact that the Democrats had achieved and were maintaining a rare degree of unity, and the further fact that, with respect to some matters of fundamental importance to the national well-being, they gave Eisenhower stronger support than he could count on receiving from many Republican Senators.

The Johnson pattern retained its effectiveness. In fact, it worked even better in this session than in the preceding one. There was no longer any necessity for him to prove himself in the leadership. Nobody was talking these days about "political bankruptcy" for the Democratic Party.

Johnson was by no means unmindful of the congressional elections coming up in November. His efforts as Minority Leader in the Senate were directed at building a Democratic record on which Democratic candidates for Congress could successfully contend for victory at the polls.

As a Democrat in a position of leadership, he was convinced the greatest service he could render his party was to guide it into and along the path of moderation. He believed the party had made great strides in regaining much of the respect it had lost during the years when it was veering off to the left. He wanted to hold those gains and add to them.

"Eventually," he said, "the people will reject any political organization that is ruled by the extremists, either of the right or the left. If I can leave any imprint on the Democratic Party, I want it to have the effect of making ours a moderate party, not a party of extremes."

He succeeded in making the issue of the 1954 campaign the "politics of responsibility" record of the Democrats in Congress.

Johnson was an exceedingly active participant. He made a whirlwind campaign through the nine states of Colorado, Washington, Montana, Wyoming, Utah, Nevada, Arizona, New Mexico and Minnesota. His basic theme was the need for formulating a national program that "would advance the interests of America, regardless of party."

He said the Republicans were concentrating on the "myth" that there would be a "cold war," which would stymie the legislative process, if a Democratic Congress should be elected. "If there is any cold war, the Republicans will have to start it themselves," he declared. "We Democrats will be too busy trying to transact the nation's business.

"However," he added, "I can well understand why the Republicans are so quick to accept the cold war interpretation of American politics. They have been carrying on that kind of war among themselves for the past two years. It seems only natural to them that they will have to carry on such a war against the Democrats."

When he returned to Texas at the end of his campaign tour, Johnson predicted the Democrats would win both houses of Congress. The Republicans, he said, would have no one but themselves to blame for such an outcome.

"The basic issue which has stirred the American people," he continued, "is the inability of Republican legislators to cooperate with the President, the American people, or with one another. The overwhelming desire of Americans is for a responsible Congress which will transact the people's business with a minimum of showmanship and a maximum of efficiency."

A few days after the election, which gave the Democrats control of Congress (although by only one seat in the Senate), Johnson went to Washington, where the Senate was to meet for the purpose of considering the resolution proposing censure of Joe McCarthy. He held a news conference soon after his arrival. Representatives of press, radio and television jammed his office to hear him explain what the Democrats would do in the new Congress.

In a formal, although unwritten, statement and in response to reporters' questions, he outlined a picture of what could be expected.

First of all, he made it clear that the Democrats would not go into the coming session "in a belligerent frame of mind. On the contrary," Johnson earnestly assured the news gatherers, "we will go into that session with a pledge of cooperation from our side and a plea for cooperation from the other side. We will be willing and eager to meet the President more than halfway."

He said: "There need be no legislative stalemate. There need be no controversy for the sake of partisan controversy."

He expressed the opinion that the closeness of the election results showed that "The American people rejected extreme partisan appeals" and "voted on a highly selective basis."

"I believe," he said, "they are looking to members of both parties in Congress to put the national welfare first, and partisan considerations a very low second. The Democrats in Congress are going to do their best to live up to this expectation of the people."

Having thus made it plain that the Democrats still rejected the "cold war" idea, he went ahead to announce that a meeting would be held shortly of members of the Senate Democratic Policy Committee along with those Democrats who would take over as committee chairmen in the new Congress. By the time the congressional session convened in January, he said, details of the legislative program to be proposed by the Democratic majority would have been thoroughly worked out.

"This will be a constructive program, tailor-made to fit the present needs of the nation," he stated. "It will deal with issues vital to the continued security and progress of the United States. I mean such issues as an enlightened foreign policy, an adequate defense program, and domestic policies designed to pass the basic test of what is best for Americans generally.

"President Eisenhower has said that he is determined to be the President of all Americans. I see no reason why a Democratic Congress and a President holding to that objective should not be able to work together in harmony on such issues as those I have mentioned."

Johnson explained, too, that the Senate leadership was working closely with the House leadership. He had stopped off in Bonham, Texas, on his way to Washington for a conference with Rayburn, who once again would assume the House Speakership in January.

"This entire program will be coordinated through the Senate Democratic Policy Committee and the leadership organization of the House of Representatives," he said. "Out of deference to the President, the program will not be presented until we have heard his State of the Union message. We hope there will be few points of difference."

He was following his usual policy of touching all the bases. The few remaining weeks of the year were crammed with conferences and planning for the Majority Leader role he would assume in the Eighty-fourth Congress.

· XI ·

Johnson was now forty-six years of age, the youngest man ever to serve as Senate Majority Leader of either party. Even so, he could look back on some twenty-two years of experience in government and eighteen years of service in Congress. His black hair was beginning to gray and to slip back in front, and a few lines had appeared on his keen face. These outward evidences of maturity were more than matched by the knowledge he had gained about how to get things done in the Senate.

He faced the job ahead of him with undisguised relish. He conceived of it primarily as a sort of general managership. As a matter of fact, floor leaders were officially known as managers in the early days of Congress. Then, as now, the man holding the majority post in the Senate had the responsibility of managing procedures there and keeping the legislative process in as smooth-flowing motion as possible. It was no kind of work for a lone operator, but Johnson had never been one and now he threw himself more than ever into cooperative endeavor.

During the first six months of 1954, his desk in the Senate was the focal point of the chamber. That was where the signals were called.

Men came to his desk who seemed to have little more in common than the fact that all were United States Senators: Byrd of Virginia, whose inborn conservatism truly represented the squirearchy of his state; sharp-tongued Wayne Morse, the eternal rebel from Oregon; Minority Leader Knowland, stubborn and dependable; fast-talking Hubert Humphrey, with an opinion on everything and a superb facility in expressing all his opinions; Leverett Saltonstall, whose very appearance spoke in modulated tones of his Massachusetts background—these and many others.

"Come, now," Johnson said to these men, "and let us reason together!"

He was the manager and he managed, not in the sense of bossing, but in the sense of coordinating, of deciding who would take the lead in regard to a specific bill, of bringing men and their ideas together.

If he was accused of compromising in order to reach agreement, he retorted that history showed American democracy was born in compromise and depends, for its effective functioning, on the give-and-take of friendly men who respect one another's integrity and refrain from questioning one another's motives.

If newspaper columnists, who thrived on controversy, complained that the Senate machinery was working *too* smoothly, he voiced his conviction that the American people wanted their government to operate quietly and efficiently. "I don't think they want anybody to rock the boat just for the fun of it," he declared.

If some of the fringe organizations that were dogmatic

about their self-advertised liberalism accused the Majority Leader of "betraying great principles" and "abandoning the true Democrats," Johnson said nothing. But he would be on the Senate floor to listen when a Senator of whom the complaining group highly approved stood up to defend his leadership.

In keeping the business of the Senate moving along, he worked most closely with Knowland. Agreement between the two on legislative procedure—regarding which bills would be taken up on a certain day and which held over—was a necessity.

"There never was a motion made to proceed to consideration of a bill that Bill Knowland didn't have his initials on," Johnson said later in reviewing the session. "There were no surprises. There were no tricks. There was no hot-airing."

Johnson's method of operation was to grease the skids before a bill ever reached the Senate for action. This process began with the committees. He constantly insisted that his committee chairmen and their members give full attention to their homework on every bill referred to them. When an item of proposed legislation was referred to the Senate, he wanted to have available every last pertinent fact about it.

He kept a running check on the sentiment of Democratic Senators regarding controversial legislation. When the time came for a vote, he was almost always able to predict what the outcome would be. And, of course, if he felt the outcome was not going to be to his liking, the time did not come for a vote until after he had exerted his powers of persuasion to their fullest extent.

Sometimes he used more than persuasion. Once, when he thought the vote on a pending bill was going to be about as close as possible, he managed to defer the roll call until a Democratic member, who had been out of town, arrived by air at National Airport and was rushed to the Capitol with a motorcycle escort. Incidentally, Johnson had counted heads too pessimistically this time. He had several more votes than he needed.

In considering Administration proposals, the Democrats held steadfastly to the policy of responsibility they had adopted when they were in the minority.

When the President submitted the Formosa Resolution, serving notice on the Chinese Communists not to advance against the Nationalists on the Island of Formosa, it was Johnson who took the lead in urging its approval.

Later, as the President was preparing to go to the Geneva Conference, Johnson jumped on a resolution by Joe McCarthy which would have hamstrung the Chief Executive in dealing with the Russian leaders. The Majority Leader adroitly forced Knowland, Hickenlooper of Iowa and other onetime McCarthy supporters to help nail down the coffin lid. The Senator from Wisconsin was able to muster only three votes besides his own in support of his resolution.

Johnson did more than any other man in the Senate to get legislation for Eisenhower's world trade program out of the Finance Committee, of which he was a member, and through the Senate in an acceptable form.

Nothing was happening to bear out the prediction made in the 1954 campaign that election of a Democratic Congress would give birth to a regressive "cold war" between the executive and legislative branches of the government.

Reviewing such instances of Democratic cooperation with the Administration, columnist Walter Lippmann, an outspoken admirer of the President, commented: "I do not think it is any exaggeration to say that Mr. Eisenhower's success as President began when the Republicans lost control of Congress and the standing committees. In his first two years he had suffered an almost unbroken record of frustration and of domination by the senior Republicans, and particularly the Republican committee chairmen in the Senate."

Inevitably, there was some criticism of any Democratic cooperation at all with the President. The left-wing Americans for Democratic Action, for example, accused Johnson of acquiescing in a Republican "assault on liberalism." But the blast was promptly answered by a former ADA president, Hubert Humphrey.

Humphrey took the floor of the Senate to defend the integrity of Johnson's own liberalism and praised the Majority Leader as "a genius in the art of the legislative process." As for himself, he said, "I have no hesitation in saying that I am proud of the leadership and of the skills portrayed by the Senator from Texas."

Senator Richard Neuberger of Oregon, a new member of the Senate's "liberal bloc" and one for whom Johnson had campaigned in 1954, also made it clear that he did not agree with the ADA's criticism of the Majority Leader. "I think Johnson is as liberal as he can be and still continue as the effective leader of the Senators who sit on the Democratic aisle of the Senate," Neuberger said bluntly.

Traditional Democratic causes were not being deserted by Johnson. No presidential proposals received automatic approval from the Senate Democrats. Each one was subjected to a searching examination.

When the Democrats disliked what such an inspection revealed, they endeavored either to kill the proposal or to bring about the modifications they wanted. Most often they were successful.

The President asked for an increase in the minimum wage rate from seventy-five to ninety cents. The Democrats insisted on and obtained a dollar.

The Senate followed Johnson's counsel in throwing out the President's highway aid bill and passing one of its own.

The President asked for a 6 per cent pay increase for postal workers. The Senate voted a raise of 8 per cent after Eisenhower had vetoed a slightly higher increase, and the President signed the Senate's bill.

The Democrats believed the Eisenhower-approved housing bill did too little about slum clearance. They rammed through a measure authored by one of their own, John Sparkman of Alabama, which provided for more slum clearance.

It was not surprising that some observers said the theme song the Democrats tauntingly rendered to the

Administration had the refrain, "Anything you can do, I can do better."

Day and night Johnson courted and cajoled his slim majority. He was now reaping the benefits of the exhaustive spadework he had done for two years as Minority Leader. The Senate was by no means a one-man band under Johnson's direction, but there was never any doubt at all about who was the leader of the band.

His deliberate purpose, as summarized by Arthur Krock of *The New York Times*, was to make campaign issues "the business of the titular party leaders and the national committees," with members of Congress left free to devote themselves solely to considering legislation, "preferably," Krock added, "on its merits." In following this policy, Johnson considered that he was simultaneously serving both his country and his party.

"The Democratic Party is big enough for all men who believe in doing what's best for America," he proclaimed in an address in the spring of that year. "There are divergent views about how best to accomplish that.

"I believe good Democrats should stress and emphasize areas of agreement. They can meet on more things than they can divide on. There are times when they must divide; but when they do, it must be on the basis of conviction, not personality.

"There are many things advanced in the name of the Democratic Party I am unable to embrace and subscribe to. But a party, like a country, is subject to the rule of the majority.

"When I find I don't subscribe to the views of some

of the party's leaders, I differ with dignity and with whatever effectiveness I can muster.

"I ask no Democrat to embrace everything I believe in and I reserve the same right for myself.

"But I'll say this," the Senate Democratic Leader concluded firmly. "The Democratic Party at its worst is better for the country than the Republican Party at its best."

It was a statement giving notice to members of both parties that he was and would remain a staunch partisan, even though he stood ready to subordinate partisanship to other considerations when the facts warranted such action.

In such statements as this Johnson gave repeated proof that he was still the man with a purpose. He was determined that he would spare no effort to cause members of his party and, so far as possible, all Senators to labor cooperatively to advance the national welfare. And his immediate object was to bring about passage of legislation in this session that would reflect justified credit on the congressional majority.

If he felt the occasion demanded, Johnson could always obtain a solid, or nearly solid, Democratic vote in the Senate. He had an uncanny ability for winning the close ones. As the session glided onward and Capitol Hill newsmen became aware of the kind of record the Democratic majority was making in dealing with a Republican Administration, the reporters began to ask Johnson how he could so consistently carry along with him a majority composed of such dissimilar elements.

"I don't carry them along," Johnson answered. "When the Democrats vote together, they do so because each man has become convinced he should vote that way.

"Most of the credit for this convincing belongs to our committee chairmen. This Senate has the master craftsmen of all time in charge of the committees. That's where the most important work is done, and there has never been a Senate that has had men who were more experienced in the subject matters with which they deal than this one."

His committee chairmen, Johnson pointed out, were "old pros." Some of them had been in the Senate fifteen, twenty, even twenty-five years or more. Even the younger ones among them mostly had imposing records of public service. They knew their subjects, whether defense or finance, housing or agriculture or foreign policy, world trade or labor. When problems came up in any governmental field, they understood how to find out the answers. They worked hard and, since they were professionals, they worked without any wasteful spinning of wheels.

That was Johnson's answer to questions about the "Why?" of Senate efficiency. Its accuracy was borne out by the results. And, of course, as Stewart Alsop explained in his syndicated newspaper column, Johnson himself was an "old pro." Said Alsop:

"There is always something peculiarly satisfying about watching a genuine professional at work, whether on the baseball diamond or on the floor of the United

States Senate. Anyone who wants to see in action the best professional Floor Leader of our time need only visit the Senate gallery at a tense legislative moment and keep his eye on the tall, lanky, slow-moving form of the Majority Leader as he ambles about on the floor below.

"Like a great professional athlete, Lyndon Johnson of Texas makes no wasted motion. A word here and there, a casual political arm around a recalcitrant shoulder, a brief, companionable colloquy with his opposite number, William Knowland of California, and the chances are that the bill under consideration will slide through the Senate almost without debate."

Exactly that happened time and again during the first session of the Eighty-fourth Congress. The Senate, under Johnson's calming guidance, not only had a new dignity and friendship but also had a new, swift pace. Bills were rarely buried in committees. There were no filibusters, no night sessions. The Senate was in session about two-thirds as long, measured in legislative hours, as the comparable session of the Eighty-third Congress. But the box score of achievement was impressive. In bringing an atmosphere of moderation and a willingness to give and take into the Senate, Johnson had turned it into a house of unusual accomplishment.

He was frankly proud of what had been done. The record, he felt, more than justified the policy he had set up as a guiding star for the Democratic majority.

At the end of June, when it was generally agreed that Congress would adjourn in another comparatively easy thirty days, Johnson was putting out at weekly intervals a list of the principal accomplishments of the session. Six weeks after the session ended, a complete digest of legislative action was compiled by his staff and printed as a Senate document, along with a statement by Johnson.

This statement, giving as it does an accounting of his stewardship during his first year as Majority Leader, has a significance justifying its reproduction in full. It is a summing up of the legislative record of the Democratic Congress during the third year of the Eisenhower Administration. It also sets forth in abbreviated form Johnson's basic governmental philosophy.

The statement follows:

"The first session of the Eighty-fourth Congress can rightly claim credit for many achievements.

"Its deliberations were conducted in the workmanlike, efficient manner that befits prudent legislators.

"It passed many measures designed to promote and preserve the prosperity of workers, farmers and businessmen.

"It put to rest the fears of those who had so little confidence in the American system they thought it would not work unless the Congress and the Executive were controlled by the same political party.

"But the crowning achievement of the session was to unite the nation behind a policy designed to protect our freedoms and preserve peace. The voices of discord were reduced to a minimum and the preservation of America was given priority over petty partisanship.

"From a statistical standpoint, the record is impressive. There were no all-night sessions; no overextended debates; no exhausting arguments to leave heated passions smoldering. Nevertheless, more responsible and thorough work was done than in many, many years.

"A comparison of this session with the first session of the Eighty-third Congress illustrates the point. This session passed about 30 per cent more bills in about 30 per cent less time; it left fewer measures hanging on the calendar and fewer measures lost in committee files; it confirmed nearly forty thousand presidential nominations as compared to about 23,500 during the first session of the Eighty-third Congress.

"Furthermore, this Senate session tackled important and highly controversial legislation—minimum wage, public housing, upper Colorado River project, long-range trade program. No one of these bills took longer than three days to pass.

"But the box score—as a measure of achievement—is inadequate, standing alone. Lists of bills which were —and were not—passed are interesting topics for study. But the real test of a Congress is whether it met the problems before the people in a spirit of prudence and a spirit of patriotism.

"By this standard, the first session of the Eighty-fourth Congress can submit its record to the people without hesitation.

"This session demonstrated that national unity can be achieved in the field of foreign policy when men put national interest above partisan interest.

"The objectives of foreign policy should be to promote and preserve the security and the integrity of the

United States. From the very beginning of this Congress, the Democratic leadership made it clear that they would support the President in any effort to obtain those objectives.

"That promise was fulfilled.

"It was fulfilled in the Formosa Resolution when the President sought to draw a line against Chinese Communist aggression.

"It was fulfilled in the approval of the Paris pacts, which laid the cornerstone for the defenses of Europe against communism.

"It was fulfilled in the ratification of the Austrian Treaty, which set the stage for the Big Four conference.

"It was fulfilled during the Big Four conference itself when the Democratic leadership unhesitatingly endorsed the President's disarmament inspection proposal.

"The future of the nation was at stake. This Congress —unlike some of its predecessors—thought that in such times the country should be united rather than divided.

"For this achievement, a major share of the credit should go to the senior Senator from Georgia, Walter F. George. As chairman of the Senate Foreign Relations Committee, he spoke with the authentic voice of America and had as much to do with shaping our policies as any other man.

"But the credit can be shared by many in varying degrees. The unmistakable fact is that unity was established—by agreement and not by coercion—and the nation was strengthened against the trials that lie ahead.

"This session also ruled out the floor of the Senate

as a partisan arena for harassing a President just before he sets out to attend a conference with the heads of foreign states. This is a precedent which could well be studied by others.

"In terms of quality, the legislative standards of this session were high. Able and experienced leaders like Senators Clements of Kentucky, George of Georgia, Fulbright of Arkansas, Hayden of Arizona, Hill of Alabama, Magnuson of Washington, and others insisted upon thorough, but expeditious, consideration of bills.

"Some of the measures made headlines, such as the trade program, the Reserve bill, the housing bill, the minimum wage bill, and Federal pay legislation. Others —fully as important—did not receive as much attention but shared equally in making up the character of this Congress.

"Interest rates were reduced on farm loans and programs were instituted to cushion the shock to agriculture of natural disasters. The penalties were increased for anti-trust violations and greater protections against market manipulations were enacted for the commodity exchanges.

"A commission was established to make a thorough overhaul of the Federal security program—a long overdue step. A tax loophole was closed which would have cost the Treasury at least a billion dollars.

"These are only a few of the bills that were passed— bills designed to help Americans individually and collectively.

"This session conducted itself in the finest traditions

of responsible legislative conduct. The President's recommendations were considered thoroughly and examined from the standpoint of how they fitted into the needs of the country. In many cases they were improved; in some they were passed practically without change; in others they were not acted upon at all. In short, Congress did not conduct itself as a rubber stamp but discharged its constitutional obligation of representing the American people.

"In no case was the Senate floor turned into a political convention or a political ward meeting at a time when the Senate was scheduled to consider legislation.

"There will, of course, always be arguments as to the measures that the Senate did or did not pass. But those arguments are inevitably matters of judgment. The Senate is responsible to the people of the country and only to the people of the country. It is not an adjunct of the Executive or the Judiciary but an independent body elected to represent the will of the people.

"There can be only one judge of success or failure, and that is the people themselves."

This statement was issued in mid-September. Meanwhile, Johnson had suffered the heart attack that took him out of action during the last month of the congressional session. But, so far as the Senate was concerned, it was still his session and the pride he felt in its accomplishments was deeply personal.

· XII ·

Each daily session of the United States Senate is opened with a prayer either by the Chaplain or a visiting minister. When the Senate convened on Tuesday, July 5, 1955, Chaplain Frederick Brown Harris offered a prayer which concluded with these words:

"We think this day with tender solicitude of the stalwart leader in this body who so recently spoke from his place of high responsibility with passion and deep sincerity regarding pending public questions. Now that suddenly he has been stricken, in this time of anxiety we pray for his family watching by his side.

"In Thy will we lift our petition that the dedicated skill of physicians and the ministry of nurses may soon restore him to his dear ones and to his place in the councils of the nation in this crucial day. Guide his colleagues upon whom for the time the mantle rests.

"May each of us in his place where we stand do our best as each day beckons, knowing that the night cometh when our work will be done. Amen."

For two days newspapers and the air waves had carried bulletins about Johnson's heart attack and attendant developments. But there had been no official statement from attending physicians beyond the initial announcement that the attack was "moderately severe." Now, as Acting Majority Leader Earle C. Clements obtained recognition from the President of the Senate to offer a statement, Senators all over the chamber turned their heads to listen with serious interest.

Clements told briefly how Johnson had suffered the attack at the beginning of what was to have been a week-end of rest. He then read a statement prepared by Dr. James Cain, a Mayo Brothers physician and long-time friend of the Johnson family who had flown to Washington to consult with the attending physicians.

The statement, short and to the point, was more reassuring than not:

"Senator Lyndon B. Johnson has had a myocardial infarction of a moderately severe character. He was quite critically ill immediately following the attack but his recovery has been satisfactory.

"His physicians agree that under no circumstances can he return to his duties during this session. He cannot undertake any business whatsoever for a period of months.

"However, if there are no further attacks of a severe character and his recovery continues to be satisfactory, he should be able to return to the Senate in January."

Clements made no attempt to interpret this statement. Having read it, he went on to give such details as he knew about Johnson's condition. The stricken man was allowed no visitors other than his wife, who had moved into the hospital to be with him. Johnson's mother had flown to Washington from Austin—the first airplane trip of her life. Johnson was said to be resting comfortably. He was, however, still in an oxygen tent.

"Under the circumstances," the Kentucky Senator continued, "it becomes my duty, as Acting Majority Leader, to assume his responsibilities. I have no hesitancy in confessing that it is difficult and disturbing to step into the shoes of such a man, even though my tenancy is only temporary.

"During this session, Lyndon Johnson has set standards of leadership that have won him the deserved acclaim of all who are devoted to democratic ideals of government. His hard work and his timely efforts have reflected credit not only upon him but upon the entire Senate.

"As a close personal friend, I am deeply devoted to Lyndon Johnson. As an American citizen, I am proud of the opportunity to be associated with him in any capacity.

"I doubt," Clements said earnestly, "if there is a member of the Senate, on either side of the aisle, who does not look upon Lyndon Johnson as a friend."

What followed immediately was testimony enough to the accuracy of the Kentuckian's estimate of Johnson. Clements' statement touched off a chain reaction as Democratic and Republican Senators sought for suitable words to express their deep personal feeling about the Majority Leader.

Lehman of New York, who had so often crossed swords with Johnson on party policy, proposed a resolution "That the Senate stand in silent prayer to the Almighty for the early and complete recovery of the Majority Leader, the beloved senior Senator from Texas." In an unprecedented action, all members and all other occupants of the chamber stood together in silence as each individual offered his own prayer.

A constantly recurring theme in the remarks of the Senators who spoke that day was the spirit of friendship and dedicated endeavor that Johnson had brought to the work of the Senate. It was this spirit which Clements pledged himself to maintain to the best of his ability. In that endeavor Minority Leader Knowland gave assurance he would cooperate fully.

Democrats like Chavez, Symington, Ellender, Humphrey, Mansfield, Hill, Gore and Monroney were joined by such Republicans as Karl E. Mundt of South Dakota, Margaret Chase Smith of Maine and Thomas K. Kuechel of California in praising both the leadership ability and the personal qualities of the man who had loomed so large in the Senate during that session. The sometimes vitriolic Wayne Morse spoke movingly of Johnson's unselfishness and of his personal debt to the fallen leader. "During the past year, I have been the beneficiary of one kindness after another from Lyndon Johnson," Morse said with emotion. "I consider him not only a great statesman, but a good man."

There was nothing formalized about the tributes. They were spontaneous expressions coming from the hearts of those who gave voice to them.

More than one Senator stated his agreement with

Alben Barkley's thought: "I believe the greatest tribute all of us can pay to him in the Senate is to cooperate in carrying forward the necessary business of the Senate for the remainder of this session, and not to allow it to lag in any way."

That was spoken out of a deep understanding of Johnson and his feeling about the work of the Senate.

It was not surprising that the Senators, who worked with Johnson and saw him in action every day, realized that in him they had a leader who deserved tremendous respect. What *was* somewhat surprising, however, even to those who knew the Texan best, was the evidence which accumulated rapidly that the value of his leadership was recognized throughout the nation.

This was first shown in the flood of newspaper editorial comment that came in the days following his heart attack. At times it seemed to Johnson's office staff, as they opened the incoming mail, that every newspaper editor in the country had been keeping an eye on the Democratic Leader's work and was now determined that his readers should share in their knowledge of that work and the man who had done it.

There were hundreds of editorials. They appeared in newspapers in every state and in Canadian and English publications. Taken as a whole, they provided incontrovertible proof that Johnson's policy of "unity—moderation—cooperation" was more deeply representative of popular sentiment in the United States than even he could have guessed.

A "composite" editorial, made up of one sentence from each of a score of editorials appearing in representative American newspapers, follows:

"Lyndon Johnson, Majority Leader in the Senate, has proved to be one of the born leaders. (Canton, Ohio, *Repository*.) The 46-year-old Texan has distinguished himself as an astute and conscientious composer of differences not only between a Democratic Congress and a Republican Executive but also among factions of Democrats. (Portland *Oregonian*). In the Majority Leadership he has revealed authentic genius. (Louisville *Times*.)

"The leadership provided by Senator Johnson in a Democratic-controlled, though closely divided, Senate in the midst of a Republican Administration has been notable for the smoothness of its functioning, the absence of caviling and obstructionist tactics and the harmony which has been induced within his own traditionally wide-split party. (Columbus, Ohio, *State Journal*.) He made an outstanding record in welding party unity among liberal and conservative Democrats. (*Labor*, Washington, D. C.)

"The Johnsonian leadership has been almost matchless in terms of tactical skill and in giving the Democrats a new unity on almost every occasion. (*New York Times*.) Mr. Johnson has won the respect of legislators in both parties as a capable and devoted officer of Congress. (New York *Herald Tribune*.) One of the ablest members of either branch, the Texan is largely responsible for the dispatch with which the Eighty-fourth

[146]

Congress has been doing its work. (St. Louis *Post-Dispatch*.) He pushed through needed legislation in the interest of the nation rather than of any one party. (Stamford, Connecticut, *Advocate*.)

"Lyndon Johnson has been the leader—one might say—of the Republican as well as of his own party. (New York *Mirror*.) In matters of legislation, he has been more the President than Eisenhower. (St. Petersburg, Florida, *Times*.) He has become one of the most influential men in the political life of the nation. (Dallas *News*.)

"If the country is now traveling on a course of pleasant waters approximating an era of good feeling, a very considerable share of the credit belongs to Senator Johnson. (Providence *Bulletin*.) By tact, good will and level headedness, he has managed to work with the Republican President and to make a good record for his Party, too. (Washington *Star*.)

"Serving in what is undoubtedly the most exacting role on Capitol Hill, he has shown a parliamentary brilliance and a talent both for composing intraparty differences and for expediting the business of the Senate that has rarely been matched in recent years. (Buffalo *News*.) The first session of the Democratic-controlled Eighty-fourth Congress was really Johnson's session. (*Life Magazine*.)

"The nation needs Lyndon Johnson. (Amarillo, Texas, *News*.) He has the makings of a statesman. (Greenville, South Carolina, *Piedmont*.) A nation which needs his kind of leadership in its legislative halls will hope that the strength of heart he has shown in the political arena will serve to pull him through this greatest crisis in his life and restore him to full vigor. (Beaumont, Texas, *Enterprise*.)

"We join with the President and the Senate in wishing Senator Johnson a prompt and complete recovery. (Phoenix, Arizona, *Republic*.)"

The Senators respected Johnson's ability and liked him personally. The newspaper editors approved of his policies and admired the way he put those policies into effect.

The people, it turned out, just plain loved Lyndon Johnson.

Within hours after the first announcement was made of Johnson's heart attack, messages for him began to flood the hospital. They came at first by telephone and telegraph and then, after a couple of days, also by mail. They came not only from longtime friends and Texas political supporters but also from figures high in the government and business worlds and from other people of whom Johnson had never heard and who he would have said could never have heard of him.

"Get well," the messages said. "The nation needs you."

"I had a heart attack myself years ago," many of them said. "You can be good as new if you will do thus and so."

"We read in the newspapers how you work for the whole country and not just for the Democratic Party," they said. "That's what we want. You get well and keep it up."

"We are praying for you," said thousands of messages.

Anxious telephone calls were followed by letters from the President and all members of his Cabinet, the Vice-President, nearly every Senator and many members of the House of Representatives, governors and ambassadors. Bernard Baruch sent his good wishes, and so did Audie Murphy and Walter Winchell and Adlai Stevenson and Jimmy Byrnes, Herbert Bayard Swope, Governor Averell Harriman of New York and Governor Allan Shivers of Texas.

And the president of Wiley College for Negroes in Marshall, Texas, near the community where Lady Bird was brought up, wrote that the students there were praying for Johnson's recovery.

Clare Boothe Luce, Ambassador to Italy and a former colleague of Johnson in the House of Representatives, sent two messages to express her concern.

And an elderly lady, an old-age pensioner who described herself as among the many who had been helped by Johnson's efforts in Congress, enclosed a dollar bill with her letter. She said she knew how much it could mean to receive a dollar unexpectedly in the mail and she thought perhaps the money would buy something he wanted for his hospital room.

General Lucius Clay, who had been largely responsible for the content of the Eisenhower highway bill which Johnson had so roundly trounced in the Senate a little while before, wrote several pages in longhand to express his admiration for the man from Texas.

And a letter from an organization of Catholic Sisters told Johnson that he had been adopted as their personal Senator, with daily prayers being said for him.

A German lawyer wrote—in German—that he had once suffered a heart attack, knew how to expedite recovery, and was willing to come to the United States at his own expense to pass on his knowledge "because of what you, as a leader in your country, have done for my country."

And an Indiana farmer and his wife sent a different greeting card every day for three weeks, each bearing a handwritten verse of comforting and applicable Scripture.

The typed and penciled letters, the post cards, the "Get well" greeting cards and the gifts—books, flowers, special foods, a tiny radio set, a handmade "prayer handkerchief," and dozens of other items—came from all sections of the country and from virtually every state. They came from all kinds of people, rich, poor and in-between: housewives, farmers, corporation presidents, laborers, bankers, old-age pensioners, clubwomen.

Johnson had developed into a popular national figure without himself realizing it. His heart attack had come at the precise time that the country was learning of his outstanding job as Majority Leader, and of the policies which were enabling him to do that kind of job. With the newspapers and radio and television now pouring out an endless fountain of information about him, the people learned more and liked what they learned.

One of the Washington newspaper writers headed a column, "Everybody Loves Lyndon." That seemed to sum up the situation fairly enough.

· XIII ·

Within two weeks from the time he entered the hospital Johnson had his recovery effort organized like one of his political campaigns and, characteristically, was giving it all he had.

He did everything the doctors told him to do, adhering to his long-established policy of obtaining the best advice possible and then following it. That policy had paid off in politics. He had no doubt it would work as well in this fight for life and health. In fact, he was soon trying to go the doctors one better. He added a few trimmings of his own to the regimen they ordered for him.

Once a fervent French fried steak and potatoes man, his daily intake of calories was now limited by the doctors to fifteen hundred—and by himself to twelve hundred. The doctors wanted him to reduce his weight from two hundred to a hundred and eighty-five pounds. He announced his own determination to cut the figure ten pounds below that goal.

Once a chain smoker, he now gave up cigarettes completely. But he kept a package on a bedside table at all times as a means of testing himself.

Once inclined to flare up in quickly passing irritation over trifles, he now refused to become disturbed if things went a little wrong. He suffered two periods of the deepest depression during the early stages of his recovery, but they passed as he gained ground in the battle—and everything was always a battle for Johnson —to achieve greater serenity of spirit.

He even took long naps each afternoon, a development which anyone who knew him would have taken oath was impossible.

He had help. Lady Bird had moved into the hospital the night her husband was brought there, and she stayed until he was discharged five weeks later. She was given a room next to him. For the first few critical days there was never a time when she was more than a few feet away from him.

"Every time I lifted my hand," Johnson later recalled gratefully, "she would be there."

She took charge of his diet, figuring it out calorie by calorie, with full regard to nutritive value and vitamins. As Johnson began to improve, he was allowed a few carefully rationed visitors, and Lady Bird again did the rationing. She read to her husband the thousands of encouraging messages that poured in. She answered them all, dictating letters for a couple of hours before her patient woke up in the morning and signing letters for a couple of hours after he went to sleep at night.

Through it all she remained calm, cheerful and outwardly serene. She never lost patience. Only once, in a casual comment to her husband, did she reveal the strain she was under. "When this is over," she said quietly, "I want to go off by myself and cry for about two hours."

Close friends of the Johnsons had always maintained that Lady Bird was as remarkable in her way as Lyndon was in his. If any proof of that were needed, Lady Bird furnished it during this time. It was a period in which the pleasant Southern woman showed the kind of tempered steel that lay beneath the velvet exterior of her personality.

Johnson's mother also was on the scene during the early stages of his fight back from the heart atack. The redoubtable Rebekah Baines Johnson, now seventy-four years old, brought the valuable assets of her orderly mind and calm common sense to the atmosphere surrounding the stricken man. She charmed newspaper reporters and other callers with her stories of Johnson's boyhood, and she never wavered in her confidence that he would recover to fill the role she felt destiny still had in store for him.

His two daughters were around, too, and they brought him great comfort. Many friends came, once visitors were premitted. One of the most frequent callers was Representative Homer Thornberry, who had succeeded to Johnson's congressional seat. He was a very close friend and a longtime opponent in an endless and completely vicious series of domino games. Thornberry told Lady Bird he knew the Senator was on the upgrade when he started crowing with his oldtime lustiness over winning a game.

Johnson was able to make jokes, a little on the grim

side, about his plight. Some twelve or fourteen days after his attack Lady Bird came to his hospital room one afternoon to report that a tailor, who had been engaged to make two suits for Johnson, had called up to ask what he should do about them.

"Tell him to go ahead with the blue suit," Johnson instructed. "We can use it no matter what happens."

As he continued to improve, the visits with family and friends, the domino games and the reading proved insufficient. Two secretaries were moved out to the hospital from the senatorial office, bringing along their typewriters and their ability to remain unruffled by telephones that never stopped ringing. Walter Jenkins, Johnson's faithful and capable young "chief of staff" who had never worked for anybody else in his life, showed up two or three times daily with mail from the office and news of Senate activities. Sam Houston Johnson dug deeply into his knowledge of his brother to find ways of pleasing him and keeping him in good spirits.

The entire seventeenth floor of the hospital came to be occupied by the Johnson entourage. Hospital attachés frankly had never seen anything like it at Bethesda Naval: people coming and going, telephones ringing, typewriters rattling, and a general air of productive confusion prevailing.

All this activity was sufficiently far removed from Johnson's own room not to disturb him. But he was fully aware of the activity and was, in fact, pretty much in control of it. This was a campaign and he was running his own campaign, even though by remote control.

He made steady progress and the doctors found him a most cooperative patient.

The Senate was still in session and, although Johnson was not permitted by the doctors even to talk about legislative business, he read the *Congressional Record* every day and kept fully informed about what was going on. "Remember," he told his doctor, "my diet has always included a big helping of politics. I can't help it if I must have politics on the menu every day."

The President paid him a visit before leaving for the Geneva Conference and touched Johnson deeply by saying to him and Lady Bird, "My heart will be here with you." Vice-President Nixon came out for a talk. Sam Rayburn, having sternly waited the two weeks the doctors originally had said should elapse before Johnson had visitors outside his family, showed up to urge with fond irascibility that the patient keep in mind that he was supposed to take things easy. Senators from both parties came to the hospital, and Cabinet members and Supreme Court justices and old friends from Texas.

The expressions of concern and encouragement Johnson received from so many people were a factor of great importance in his struggle toward recovery. In a statement he gave *Roll Call*, the newspaper for Capitol Hill employees, the day after he was discharged from the hospital, he tried to tell what those messages had meant to him:

"It is trite, I suppose, to say there are a lot of good people in the world. But that is the thought which came to me over and over as I lay in my bed in Bethesda Naval Hospital fighting back toward recovery.

"In those first difficult days I was helped immeasurably by the knowledge that so many people were pulling for me and praying that I would get well. . . .

"Lady Bird, my wife, read all the comforting messages to me right from the first. I will never be able to express adequately what they did for me. I could literally feel myself gaining courage and strength from them.

"When I was discharged from the hospital, the attending physicians stated I had responded favorably to every treatment given me. Much of the credit for that circumstance belongs to the people who wired and wrote me, who left word that they were thinking of me, who sent me thousands of cheerful 'Get well' cards.

"I had always considered myself a man with an adequate appreciation of the innate goodness of humanity. I know now my appreciation was not strong enough.

"I will try earnestly never again to underestimate the kindliness and warm humanity of the American people. I will never be without a feeling of thankfulness in my heart for the way they demonstrated these inspiring traits at a time when the demonstration meant so much to me.

"My friends, known and unknown to me, sustained me when my need was great beyond description. That is why I know I am speaking the literal truth when I say, 'This is a world full of good people.'"

Visitors to the hospital and later to Johnson's Washington home, and still later to his ranch in Texas, found that he was indeed, in certain significant respects, a changed man.

"I've thrown away the whip," he told one friend. "That heart attack taught me to appreciate some things that a busy man sometimes almost forgets. I've found out it's fun to play dominoes with my two girls. I've found out again that it's pleasant to make small talk with my wife and neighbors. Essentially, it all means, I guess, that I'm learning all over how to live."

There were even deeper aspects to the change. In his rush up the political ladder, the man from Texas had never had time—or had never taken time—for serious reading and reflective thinking. He said himself that he doubted if he had read six books all the way through since leaving college. His compelling concern was always with the *now*, never with the *then*. He gained his knowledge of current issues from newspaper headlines and from memos prepared by persons whose judgment he trusted.

He had been in a mad hurry all his life. There had never been a time when he indulged in the luxury of philosophizing. In politics—and there had been little else than politics in his adult life—he acted on the basis of an instinct that very rarely led him astray. He had felt no particular need for developing a solid political philosophy, based on a well-rounded knowledge of the past as well as a keen awareness of the present.

Now, after a quarter century of hustle, bustle and rustle, Johnson was able to lean back, read, think, and arrive at conclusions that could be theoretical as well as practical in nature. The enforced leisure of his convalescence challenged him to give thought to the future of man, not just to man's daily needs.

Thus it was that people who came to see him found a Johnson who was a more reflective, more poised, quieter man than the one they had known, a Johnson who was reading Plato and early American history as well as *The New York Times* and the *Congressional Record*, a Johnson, in short, who was learning from this experience just as he had learned from every other experience of his life.

"One thing I learned for sure," Johnson told me during this period. "I learned from the letters people wrote me and from the newspaper editorials and magazine pieces that extreme, bitter-end political partisanship no longer holds an attraction for the great body of the American people.

"I am more convinced than ever that the kind of country-over-party leadership I have tried to give Senate Democrats meets the needs of the times and the wishes of the American people.

"Old-fashioned, name-calling partisanship may have been regarded in the past as a form of entertainment. It cannot be so regarded now, when the life or death of the world may hinge upon matters which must be settled by American politicians.

"I strongly believe we need an era of good feeling, politically speaking. Working together in a spirit of mutual good will, we can overcome all obstacles to our continued progress as a nation.

"That is the only way we can do it. We can't walk alone and we can't walk separately."

This was the "philosophy of moderation" that Johnson preached to high-ranking members of the Democratic Party, who came in a steady stream to visit him on his ranch in Texas in the fall of 1955. He felt that this moderate approach held the key to future success at the polls for the party. More than that, he was deeply convinced that such an approach would result in the national unity which he considered essential to continued progress and a vital factor in maintaining peace in the world.

There was much speculation among political writers for the newspapers about the extent to which Johnson was shaping Democratic Party policy. He himself disclaimed any such intention. But there was no question that in his unobtrusive, let-us-reason-together fashion he was getting over the essence of his thinking about the course the Democrats should follow.

He was the right man to do the job. As the highly respected Roscoe Drummond wrote in the New York *Herald Tribune*, "Senator Johnson's voice in Democratic matters would not be heeded the way it is now being heeded if he were primarily serving his own personal ambitions."

During all this time Johnson was applying the moderate approach to his personal life as well as advocating it as a policy of the Democratic Party. He made that clear to a friend who, commenting on the flow of newspaper stories about Johnson's important visitors, wondered if he was trying to do too much.

"No," Johnson said firmly. "The reporters tell about the visits of Adlai Stevenson, the Speaker, Bob Kerr, Hubert Humphrey and all the others. But what they don't write about is the nap I take every afternoon or how I spend my evenings quietly with Lady Bird and the girls."

He took great delight in coming really to know Lynda Bird and Lucy Baines, who were now eleven and eight years old. Johnson was charmed by their childishly serious talk of their friends, their plans for the coming school year in Washington, their pleasure in his company.

"It's funny how little things can mean so much to a man who's getting well from a serious illness," Johnson said afterward. "I learned things from those two girls in the fall of 1955 that I would never in the world have found out from anybody else.

"Why, I even learned something from our dog, Little Beagle.

"One day I was sitting out on the porch, alone and feeling rather low in my mind. I didn't say anything or do anything except maybe sort of sigh to attract Little Beagle's attention. But he suddenly got up from where he was sitting and came over to me. He put his head in my lap and just stood there, looking at me with his big eyes. 'All right, Little Beagle,' I said, 'we'll go on from here and take it as it comes.' I don't know why that

[161]

should have caused me to feel better all at once, but it did."

Among the visitors were many who had nothing to do with politics. One week-end Arthur Godfrey, a warm admirer of the Senator from Texas, gathered up a planeload of friends and flew them down to the LBJ Ranch. Newspaper people from Washington and various Texas cities dropped in to visit. His sisters and their families were around, and so was his brother, Sam Houston. A. W. Moursund, Johnson City attorney and close friend, came in often for a game of dominoes.

In spite of the comings and goings of visitors, Johnson was, for him, taking life very easily indeed. His ranch on the banks of the Pedernales River, in the picturesque hill country of Central Texas, was the ideal place for a man completing his recovery from a heart attack. The rolling land was quiet and peaceful. He saw only those persons he wanted to see, with Lady Bird fending off business calls from constituents.

For the most part his life was one of rigid routine, involving walks over the ranch in the morning, a nap every afternoon, and a great deal of lounging around in a hammock reading or listening to music from a record player.

He was still working hard at the job of getting well. "If this is a political campaign, I'll be coming up to election day in December," he said. "This is one I have to win."

In December he underwent an exhaustive series of examinations. After their conclusion the six doctors who

[162]

had treated him issued a joint statement regarding his condition. The doctors were J. Willis Hurst of Emory University at Atlanta, Georgia, a specialist who had been on active duty as a Naval Reserve officer at Bethesda when Johnson was a patient there; Howard Burchell and James C. Cain of the Mayo Clinic; Olin Grover of the excellent Scott & White Clinic at Temple, Texas; R. W. Gifford of the National Capitol Psysicians' staff, and J. B. Whaley of Johnson City.

Their statement follows:

"It has been approximately six months since Senator Lyndon B. Johnson's heart attack on July 2. We have examined Senator Johnson carefully and are in joint agreement on the following conclusions:

"(1) We are very pleased with the rapid rate of his recovery. There have been no complications and his reaction to gradually increasing activity has been favorable. His blood pressure is normal; his heart size is normal; and his electrocardiogram is that of a normal man.

"(2) Barring unforeseen complications, there is every reason for him to return to his duties and to resume major activity.

"(3) Senator Johnson, his family, his staff and his intimate friends have been advised fully of the conditions under which he can operate. These are relief from any work that can be handled just as well by his staff; carefully regulated hours of work and rest; and a frequent number of short vacations throughout the year.

"(4) Senator Johnson is generally in very good condition and fully capable of handling his duties. The sensible precautions that we have outlined for him are based upon recognition of the fact that anyone in a responsible position involving mental strain or tension should guard his health carefully."

That was that.

Johnson was very happy about this official green-light signal to resume his work in the 1956 session of Congress. Happy but not surprised. In his own mind, he felt he had known it all along.

He was prepared to observe the limitations the doctors had urged upon his activities. But he was still the Majority Leader and he knew that leadership could not be delegated. He was as ready as ever to accept its responsibilities. As the session went along, evidence mounted that his head had lost none of its wisdom, his hand none of its skill.

The Senator from Texas was still the effective leader of the majority in the United States Senate.

· XIV ·

Lyndon Johnson, in his maturity, is not the kind of politician who feels called upon to jump into any discussion around him with an expression of his own views. If he has not been able to make up his own mind on the basis of the facts available to him, he keeps quiet until he has more facts, until he has arrived at a firm conclusion.

He does hold strong views on questions of great importance to the American people. When he feels something is to be gained by setting forth these views, he does not hesitate to express them. On some subjects he has stated his position often enough and strongly enough to justify the conclusion that his approach to these subjects constitutes a major part of his fundamental political philosophy.

Here are such expressions by Johnson, excerpts from formal addresses in the Senate and elsewhere, from radio and television talks, from reports of interviews in newspapers and magazines.

* * *

[165]

On the nature of the American government:

We think of the United States as a young nation. And so it is, in many respects. Our nation is young in the vigor and progressiveness of its people—young in the history of the world—young in the sense that we look to the future, not to the past.

And yet in the field of government we cannot be accounted youthful. In fact, the United States today has the oldest unchanged form of government in the world.

Count over the nations of the world and you will realize this is true. During the span of our national existence we have seen monarchies fall, democracies born, tyrannies abolished—only to be replaced in some instances by more barbarous tyrannies.

Through it all—through wars and economic stress and changing political alignments—the United States has survived and grown stronger as a nation in which representative government has brought the blessings of freedom to all.

Our Federal government has to be big to give adequate governmental service to the people of a big nation. But it must never be allowed to become so overwhelmingly big that it swallows up the powers and responsibilities of the state and local governments.

To meet the needs of the times, our government must be strong. That strength must extend up and down the structure of our government—including the city halls and county seats and state capitals as well as the city of Washington, D. C.

There is only one source for this needed strength in government. It must come from the strength of the people—the collective power of tens of millions of individuals who are proud to call themselves Americans.

This strength can be exerted only if the people generally concern themselves with the affairs of their government. Bad government results from the indifference of good people. Our form of government depends for its continued existence upon the participation of the people.

No all-wise paternalistic government can dole out to us those blessings of life, liberty and the pursuit of happiness which our forefathers saw as the goal of the nation they founded.

Every generation of Americans must win for themselves the right to enjoy these blessings. That, indeed, is the basic meaning of the statment so frequently made that eternal vigilance is the price of liberty.

Ours is a government of, by and for the people. The *of* and *by* are no less significant than the *for*.

So, that is good government which grows out of the personal concern of individual citizens with affairs of government.

That is strong government which grows out of the united strength of a free people.

We must have this kind of good government, this kind of strong government, to insure our surviving these years of distress and danger.

It is not the kind of government that can be imposed from above. It can come only from what in our nation is, and must remain, the source of all governmental power—that is, from the people themselves.

* * *

On political partisanship:

I believe that, year in, year out, most Americans are prudent without being reactionary, progressive without being radical. That is, I think, a basic factor in the development of the United States as the great, powerful, freedom-loving nation it has become.

The American people would rather save their country than sell a doctrine. They would rather win a victory for the United States than a debate against a political opponent.

I feel that the interest of Americans in political labels is secondary. But their interest in the political principles that will serve their country's needs is primary.

I am a Democrat because I believe that in the long run the political principles of the Democratic Party best serve these national needs. That conviction runs deep with me. It has never impelled me, however, to challenge the sincerity, patriotism or good will of those who take an opposite view.

I learned early in life that a political opponent is not necessarily a horse thief. Honest and intelligent men can and do disagree. But when they are mature men, they do so without questioning each other's loyalty or good faith.

Partisanship is a basic feature of American government, but it should be partisanship based upon sincere

[168]

disagreement as to the course that is best for our nation. We are all Americans before we are members of any political party.

*　*　*

On the Democratic Party:

The Democratic Party can be a political organization of which all its adherents will be proud—not because we are Democrats but because we are Americans.

I personally believe the American people are weary of programs based upon fear. I personally believe they are sickened with politics that tests a man's loyalty by his hatred for his fellow-Americans.

They are eagerly seeking a party whose first concern is the future of our country. They are looking for leaders who want to serve because they love America— and not because they hate some of its citizens.

They long for a program of confidence and courage, not of distrust and hysteria.

That is what we must offer. That is what we will offer.

The Democratic Party is the party of all America. It is not the tool of any one section, any one class, any one group. Its doors are open to all who believe in a country whose future is unlimited.

We seek to spread—not quarantine—prosperity.

Our goal is peace in the world, not strife at home.

Our aim is the preservation of our liberties.

The American people will judge our success by our performance. And when they examine the record they

[169]

can come to only one conclusion. They will march proudly in the ranks of the Democratic Party, for the good of America.

* * *

On the role of a party Floor Leader in the Senate:

I see no difference between the responsibilities of a Majority Leader in the Senate and those of a Minority Leader, so far as party matters are concerned. In neither case is it the leader's responsibility to nominate a candidate or elect a President. He has a responsibility to his country and to the state that elects him, and his responsibility to the country and his state is to do what's right.

In doing that, of course, a party leader in the Senate can bring about a unity among rather extreme groups within the party itself. That is fitting and proper. But I have never conceived it to be the responsibility of the party leader to turn the Senate chamber into a convention hall for the purpose of nominating a President, or to turn the Senators—even if that could be done—into a bunch of precinct captains.

In frankness, I must say that, all of them being practical realists and political men, they are aware of the public reception to a public question—as they should be in a democracy. But I have never asked any member of my party, at any time, to do anything he felt he shouldn't do. As leader, I have never expected to be forced to vote with any substantial number of my colleagues just because they happen to represent a majority.

If a Majority Leader or a Minority Leader is constantly finding himself out of tune with most of the members of his party, then he probably should engage in a little introspection and submit the question of his leadership to the wishes of the majority.

But every Majority Leader has frequently found himself in the minority. He is not selected because he presents the majority views. He is selected because the other Senators of his party have confidence in him as the manager.

Both the Majority Leader and the Minority Leader owe it to the President—whether he is Republican or Democratic—to give careful, thorough consideration to the Chief Executive's recommendations. Then the leader and the other Senators have the responsibility of molding those recommendations into a form they consider calculated to serve the best interests of the people.

But the Senate Floor Leader is not working under the President, even when they belong to the same party. He is simply the leader of the Senators who named him to that position.

* * *

On world trade:

Foreign nations can buy goods produced in America only if they can pay for them in dollars. There are two ways for them to get the dollars.

One way is for our government to spend large sums of money for foreign aid programs. That is the course we followed after World War II. We literally gave away enough money to maintain our markets abroad.

The money we spent for foreign aid just about paid for the excess of our exports over our imports.

But, of course, this is something that cannot go on forever. It does not make sense to pay somebody to buy goods from us.

The other way for foreign nations to get the needed dollars is through the development of a sound trade program.

A sound trade program means a two-way trade program. In order to sell, we must be willing to buy. That is a hard economic fact. There is no way of escaping it.

Our prosperity is involved here, but not prosperity alone. Our hopes for true and lasting peace are involved. Our determination to remain a nation of free men and to aid in the spread of freedom throughout the world is involved.

We have spent billions of dollars to help our friends among the nations of the world get on their feet. It would be ironic if we undid all our work by erecting high trade walls around our borders.

If we refuse to trade—on a two-way basis, the only sound basis—with the free nations, the Communist-dominated countries will move in to fill the vacuum.

When you start tampering with tariffs, you can never foretell just who will be harmed as a result. A few American cheese producers brought pressure to limit cheese imports. The limitation was followed promptly by cancellation of French contracts for American citrus fruit. The Dutch scaled down their imports of our wheat when we limited the amount of cheese we would buy from them.

That is how it goes. Trade barriers give rise to more trade barriers.

There is a major national interest in expanding trade. Not merely the farmers, not merely a few specialized manufacturers, but all the American people will benefit from an expanding flow of world trade. In fact, all the free world will benefit.

*　　*　　*

On the nature of communism:

International communism is not merely an object of repulsion. It is a deadly threat—a threat to our lives, our liberties and our future.

It is a threat because the Communist dictators are not content to practice their tyranny in the nations they control already. They insist that their brand of dictatorship is an export commodity, a form of government that must oppose freedom wherever freedom exists.

The goal of the Communist dictators is to seize power, not by constitutional processes but by the overthrow of constitutional processes. Their objective, which they have never concealed, is a universal dictatorship ruled by themselves.

They insist that their aims are peaceful. But their whole history demonstrates that they are referring to the peace of the grave. They claim that we need not fear their aggression. But they prove—in deeds—that they merely do not want us to resist their aggression.

[173]

Our form of government is the very opposite pole of everything for which they stand.

We are a God-fearing people. They have proclaimed atheism as their sole attitude toward religion.

We believe in the dignity of the individual. They believe in the subordination of the individual to the government.

Our Constitution is based on the premise that the people must be protected against despotic rule. Their law is based on the premise that the people are forbidden to protest against despotic rule.

There can be no doubt as to their belief. They are committed to the fanatical principle that the twentieth century is the waning twilight of liberty and freedom. They are doing everything in their power to speed the approaching night.

* * *

On how to fight communism:

It has long been my belief that the greatest strength of free peoples in the struggle with communism is their unique ability and their traditional willingness to change, to adapt themselves to varying situations, to find new answers to old problems.

That is one thing that distinguishes democratic systems from totalitarian systems. Our freedom includes the right and the ability to change.

If we want to lose our freedom and lose our strength, we can do so by permitting communism to frighten us away from change.

I am not one who agrees that the active quest for peace is indicative of weakness. Only those who are strong, and who are confident of their strength, can effectively seek peace.

I believe this nation must remain sufficiently strong to sit at the conference table with Communist representatives and seek the answer to the survival of two worlds. In our foreign policy, we need and can have the combination of hardheaded realism and dynamic imagination of our forefathers.

Free men do not desire to dictate the course of allied governments or to attempt to overthrow the chosen governments of other independent nations.

Free men cannot easily guard the secrets of their strength from the eyes of enemy powers, unless they prize the secrets more highly than their freedom.

Free men cannot keep their freedom, or guarantee their security, if they attempt to keep pace in an armaments race with a totalitarian nation.

We must not deceive ourselves as to what is possible and what is not possible. We must not assume strengths where they do not exist—or weaknesses where they do not exist.

The Communist empire is vast and forbidding. It stretches across the largest land mass on the face of the globe. It has enslaved hundreds of millions of people.

But like every other structure built on fear and hate, the Communist empire has its soft spots. The most vulnerable point consists of the people themselves.

There are many men and women who have welcomed Communists into their country because they were deceived by the false promises of Marxist paradise. There are few, however—very few—who have tasted the Communist whip and do not burn with a desire to be rid of it. Even in the nations overrun and exploited by the Communists, the spirit of independence still lives and cannot be crushed completely.

We must bend our thoughts and our efforts to a search for means by which this spirit can find expression.

Preservation of freedom is everybody's business. We will all lose our liberties if we fail. We can save them only if we all work together. And nothing—absolutely nothing—can be done unless the American people understand the issues and are united.

* * *

On his faith in America:

There is no limit to the future of America but the heart and the will of her people.

Ours is a nation based upon a deep belief in ever-expanding horizons of freedom and prosperity. That belief has carried us through the storms and trials of 175 years.

We have refused to accept the boundaries set for the mind and the soul by tyranny. We have rejected the concept that mankind is doomed to destruction.

Instead, we have proclaimed the doctrine of liberty as the way of life which must and shall triumph.

Upon that foundation, we have erected a national structure which is the envy of the world. That structure will stand so long as we have the courage and confidence to match our strength.

Our factories and mills hum with productive activity.

Our people are the best fed, best clothed and best housed of any in the world.

Our children are educated not as a privilege but as a right.

Above all, we have the heritage of liberty—the right to agree or disagree with any man; to speak our minds; to choose our own government; to profess the religion of our choice.

Our responsibilities are enormous. But responsibility is only one side of a coin. The other side is opportunity, the ability to determine our own destiny.

This is the destiny of America: to lead the world, not by coercion but by example, into the age of universal freedom.

We have much to preserve, much to save.

Our soil is fertile. Our economy is strong. Our people enjoy health and prosperity.

We *will* preserve and we *will* save these blessings—because our eyes are set not upon the needs of the past but upon the accomplishments of the present and the promise of the future.

There is a vision in America, a vision that has sustained us through the years.

It is a vision of a land from which tyrants, both petty and great, have been banished.

It is a vision of a land whose people are prosperous.

It is a vision of a land which does not fear the future.

It is a vision of a land where authority is granted by—and not imposed upon—its citizens.

That vision is a reality. It will strengthen us no matter how great and overwhelming the problems we face. It will be our guiding star through the perils of the unknown.

With faith in our God and the cause of freedom, we shall march forward into a future of an ever greater and stronger America.